CONQUER LOGICAL FALLACIES

28 NUGGETS OF KNOWLEDGE TO NURTURE YOUR
REASONING SKILLS

THINKNETIC

GET 3 FREE BONUSES!

Free Bonus #1

Our Bestseller *Critical Thinking In A Nutshell*

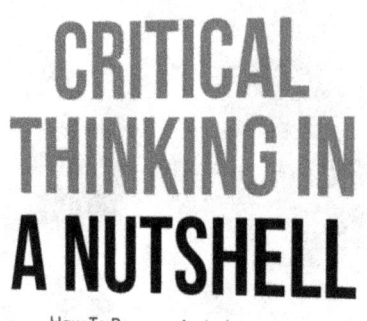

#1 Best Seller

~~$3.99~~
$0.00

Did You Know That 93% Of CEOs Agree That This Skill Is More Important Than Your College Degree?

Here's just a fraction of what you'll discover inside:

- How to shortcut the famous Malcom Gladwell "10,000 Hours Rule" to become an expert critical thinker, fast
- What a WW2 pilot and the people of Romania can teach you about critical thinking - this is the KEY to not making huge mistakes
- Actionable, easy exercises to drill home every point covered in the novel. You won't "read and forget" this book

"This book is a good primer for the beginner and a good refresh for the expert who wants to bring more critical thinking into their problem-solving. Easy to read and understand, buy this book."

(Kevin on April 19, 2021)

"This book is unlike any other on Critical Thinking. The author puts an entirely new twist in critical thinking. Very easy to understand. Give it a read and see for yourself."

(Knowledge Seeker on April 16, 2021)

"The explanations are straight forward, sensible and usable with some interesting ideas about how this can be taught or learned."

(Dave Crisp on April 14, 2021)

Free Bonus #2
Thinking Cheat Sheet *Break Your Thinking Patterns*

Free Bonus #3
Thinking Guide *Flex Your Wisdom Muscle*

Our educational system simply doesn't teach us how to think...

...and it's unlikely this is information you've ever learned anywhere else - until now.

A glimpse into what you'll discover inside:

- If your thinking is flawed and what it takes to fix it (the solutions are included)
- Tried and true hacks to elevate your rationality and change your life for the better
- Enlightening principles to guide your thoughts and actions (gathered from the wisest men of all time)

Go to thinknetic.net to download for free!

(Or simply scan the code with your camera)

SCAN ME

CONTENTS

Introduction   ix

1. To Understand Reasoning Is To First Understand Logic   1
2. Reason Through Arguments   9
3. The Culprit Of Bad Reasoning: Our Logical Errors And Biases   25
4. Demystifying The So-Called Formal Logical Errors   31
5. The Informal Logical Errors We Experience Everyday   45
6. Making The Change: How Can We Become Rational Thinkers?   115

Afterword   131
One Final Word From Us   134
Continuing Your Journey   137
The Team Behind Thinknetic   139
References   143
Disclaimer   151

INTRODUCTION

> *Men are apt to mistake the strength of their feeling for the strength of their argument. The heated mind resents the chill touch and relentless scrutiny of logic.*
>
> — William E. Gladstone

A young man and a beautiful maiden fell in love with each other, but, alas, she was a princess and he, a commoner. The king heard of this affair and, livid with rage, had the man captured and brought before him.

"You have committed an unforgivable crime and shall be executed," said the king. "But because I am a righteous and merciful king, I will allow you one kindness, and that is to choose the manner of your death. You are to make one statement. If you tell the truth, you shall be sent to the gallows to die by hanging. If you tell a lie, you will be burned at the stake. Go ahead, then. Make your statement."

The young man thought briefly, then said: "I will be burned at the stake." The king, hearing this, thought deeply, then set the man free.

Many of you readers by now will have a feeling of *déjà vu*. Of course, you had already heard this story or some variation of it sometime before. It is a version of the liar's paradox. In the story above, the young man was released by the king because his statement put the king in a quandary. If his statement was ruled a lie, he would be burned at the stake, turning his statement into the truth. But if it were the truth and he was sent to the gallows, he would have told a lie because he said he would be burned at the stake. Therefore, the righteous king, therefore, had to let him go or risk putting a man to death against the terms of his own proclamation.

The liar's paradox is a popular logical puzzle, but many who have already heard it before are again confused upon hearing it again. They could not recall the answer to this familiar story, because they would have forgotten the logical connections made before. Why? Because our human nature makes us forget what we have learned if we learned the lesson only once. Learning does not take hold if we fail to address the lesson again and to practice it repeatedly, frequently, and in different contexts.

You may be reading this book because you were intrigued by its reference to "Our Irrational Side." We are rational beings and make decisions consistent with reason and logic, but we often find ourselves caught in the repercussions of irrational actions and decisions.

- Students will forego preparing for an examination knowing full well the consequence is a failing grade. Still, they convince themselves with the fallacy that they could still pass the test by cramming or cheating.

- Employers know the opportunity cost in turning away potentially outstanding applicants because of a first impression bias, yet they repeat the habit.

- Consumers make purchases that they had no intention of making because they were swayed by celebrities and influencers posing as authorities. All of us have been there and had subsequently experienced buyers' remorse.

It is not easy to constantly think and act logically. We are the product of different cultures, experiences, educational backgrounds, and upbringing. We are each equipped with different sets of values and beliefs that combine our upbringing and social environment. Yet, logic is objective, scientific, coldly discerning. Sound reasoning often leads to one solution, the right solution.

Sound reasoning has its benefits. A right-thinking student will hit the books before an exam. Employers will recruit the best applicants based on merit after careful deliberation. And consumers will realize that models, actors, and television personalities cannot replace real engineers, physicians, and similar experts.

This book aims to help everyday people make sound everyday decisions. It discusses:

- Why people repeatedly make logical mistakes.

- What logical principles and tools can help us reason better.

- What formal and informal logical fallacies we frequently encounter, and how we can address them.

- What biases we are most prone to have, and how we can minimize them.

- What steps we can take to think logically as a habit.

The book provides a pragmatic description of the fundamental logical concepts and the most frequently encountered fallacies and biases that impact our daily decisions.

The author has a doctorate and has taught in college and graduate school for 40 years. Outside the academe, she has had field experience in business management, engineering, law, finance, and marketing. She has been married for 35 years and has raised three children, now professionals in their own right. Her wealth of experience and academic foundation enable this book's grounded approach through straightforward explanations and everyday examples.

This book is designed for the average readers who want to apply logic to their everyday lives, to tame "the heated mind" enough to relish "the chill touch and relentless scrutiny of logic." It is a journey towards mastering the skill of sound reasoning.

Are you ready to take the journey with us?

Dianna Gene P. Aquino

1

TO UNDERSTAND REASONING IS TO FIRST UNDERSTAND LOGIC

A man walks into a bar and says to his favorite bartender. "Jim, give me a stiff one. I can't stand going home to my wife this early. All she does is nag, nag, nag without making any sense, and I can't get a word in."

Jim says, "Bob, Letty's just bored. I got my Emma to attend evening classes on embroidery, and now she's too busy with her cross-stitching to get on my case." Bob thought that was a great idea.

One month later, Bob walks in and says, "Jim, this is the last time I'm listening to you. I took your advice and encouraged Letty to attend community college. She enrolled in a course on introductory logic. Now she still nags at me, and I still can't get a word in. She's making too much sense!"

Bob's experience shines a light on the best reason one can have to study logic: to persuade others with our reasoning.

Reasoning is a journey of the mind. Humans are rational beings. Therefore, we all reason. We all perceive the same things in our environment, yet we interpret them in different ways. Some interpretations make more sense than others, depending on the way we reason.

Logic is simply the process of making sense. It is the science of correct reasoning, and some would call it a discipline of the mind [1]. Some of us reason more logically than others because we can make sound inferences from the evidence we have. With study, observation, and practice, we can acquire that mental discipline to use logic to persuade and convince others effectively.

The Four Laws Of Logic

There are three classical laws of logic: the law of identity, the law of excluded middle, and the law of noncontradiction. In 1818, the German philosopher Arthur Schopenhauer introduced the fourth law, the law of sufficient reason.

The law of identity: Everything that is, exists.

The law explains that everything is identical to itself. A term used in logical discourse can refer to one and only one thing. When a term means more than one thing within the same discussion, the violation introduces a fallacy known as equivocation.

An example of equivocation is: "Jack eats what is right, and Jill eats what is left." Right means "correct" in the first half of the sentence and is implied to mean a direction in the second half. Similarly, left has a double meaning, the direction opposite to right, and the "remainder" (leftover).

The law of excluded middle: Each and every thing either is or is not.

A proposition is either true or not true. If there are two contradictory propositions, either the first is true and the second not true, or the second is true, and the first is not true. "Arthur is a faithful husband," and "Arthur had an affair while he was married." Having an affair is the definition of being unfaithful. Therefore, either it is true that Arthur is faithful and the affair did not happen, or Arthur had an extramarital affair, negating his faithfulness to his wife.

The law of non-contradiction: Nothing can simultaneously be and not be.

Contradictory propositions cannot be true at the same time and in the same sense. This is similar to the law of identity. A German shepherd cannot be a Yorkshire terrier nor a Shih-tzu (i.e., non-German shepherd). A high-rise building cannot be a bungalow (i.e., a non-high rise). But care must be taken to ensure that the propositions are truly mutually exclusionary. Benjamin Franklin is a statesman, but he is also a scientist. A scientist is not necessarily a non-statesman because being a statesman does not exclude being a scientist, and vice-versa. When two propositions can co-exist, they are not contradictory and do not violate the law of non-contradiction.

The law of sufficient reason: Of everything that is, it can be found why it is.

Of the four logical principles, this is the most controversial. It is also the most complicated, so that we will explain it with an example. Suppose Joe wanted to buy a motorcycle to get around in. A man he hardly knew approached him and said that a friend of his brother-in-law's officemate mentioned Joe's interest. The stranger will sell Joe his brand-new motorcycle for $500 if Joe makes payment in three hours.

Joe immediately jumps at the offer and says, "It's a deal!" But as a logical person, your first thought would be, "Why?" This is the gist of the fourth law. For every unexplained fact, a rational mind will seek the reason behind it. Just any reason will not do; it must be sufficient. In the example, the explanation must answer questions like: Why did the stranger want to sell it so quickly? Why at such a low price? What might be wrong with the unit? Was it contraband? Was it stolen? How did the stranger even know Joe?

Concepts Important In Logic

An appreciation of logic requires an understanding of the following concepts.

<u>Claim</u> – Also known as a statement or proposition, a claim asserts the truth or existence of something, whether true or false. When one or two premises support a claim, it becomes a conclusion.

A simple claim is an unsupported statement.

- The winner of the Miss Universe beauty contest is the most beautiful woman in the universe.

A supported statement becomes a conclusion.

- All the known women in the universe are those who live on Earth. All of these women competed in the Miss Universe pageant. Therefore, the winner of the Miss Universe beauty pageant is the most beautiful woman in the universe.

<u>Inference</u> – Inference refers to drawing conclusions from a set of information or premises and moving towards their logical consequence according to one of the recognized forms of reasoning.

The following is an example of drawing an inference through deductive reasoning.

- You asked me where I was last night, what I was doing, and who I was with. I infer from your line of questioning that you consider me a suspect.

<u>Argument</u> - An argument is a claim used to persuade or convince people regarding the truth about an issue. It has three basic elements – an issue, a premise (or premises), and a conclusion (or conclusions) [2].

While proponents use arguments to convince others, not all arguments are validly structured, and not all premises and conclusions are true. Critical thinking is required to recognize and construct a valid and sound argument, such as the following.

- Issue: How is gold traded?
- Premise 1: All precious metals are traded in the international exchanges.
- Premise 2: Gold is a precious metal.
- Conclusion: Gold is traded in the international exchanges.

Two elements necessary in reaching sound, logical conclusions are truth and honesty in reasoning. This is not easy to achieve because we tend to cloud our judgments with bias, misconceptions, and a lack of sincerity to seek out the truth. Even with the best intentions, it is sometimes difficult to dissect between truth and falsity, or honesty and insincerity, even in one's mind.

Action Steps

Try the following exercise in critical thinking, devised by Ransom Patterson, editor-in-chief of College Info Geek [3].

(1) <u>Ask basic questions</u>. Many insignificant issues may confound a problem. The first step is to eliminate the irrelevant matters that complicate the issues. Identify the basic issue and focus on its solution.

(2) <u>Question basic assumptions</u>. Assumptions are things people accept as true even without proof. Under closer scrutiny, some assumptions may be proven false or inapplicable. Learn to identify them and weigh their relevance to the problem.

(3) <u>Be aware of your mental processes</u>. Human thought happens at such speed that the brain sometimes makes mental shortcuts (heuristics) to make sense of our surroundings. Cognitive biases and personal prejudices sometimes hijack our thinking process, so it is important to guard against them.

(4) <u>Try reversing things</u>. A new perspective may emerge if one reverses what appears to be true at first. The bus may have hit the pedestrian, but the pedestrian may have intentionally stepped in front of the bus. The idea is to test the possibility of more than one explanation.

(5) <u>Evaluate the existing evidence</u>. Try to find corroboration from other sources. Exhaust all possible evidence, and the conclusion that reconciles all of them is the right conclusion. If the evidence conclusively eliminates alternatives, then the remaining alternative is the right conclusion.

These five mental exercises may seem easy, but making them a habit will take time, patience, and practice.

Developing the inclination to think critically is the first step to using logic effectively. The next step is to structure those thoughts precisely to deliver your message convincingly.

Moving On

This brief overview of logic barely scratches the surface of this most interesting topic, but it is certainly enough to give Bob goosebumps thinking about getting into an argument with his wife. Mastery of logic is a powerful weapon for winning arguments, but more so for making sound decisions. Bob would consider it a boon to study logic like Letty. And so would you. Let's forge on to the reasoning through arguments in the next chapter.

Key Takeaways

- The four laws of logic are the laws of identity, excluded middle, non-contradiction and sufficient reason.
- A claim asserts the truth of something.
- Inference is drawing conclusions from premises.
- An argument is a claim supported by proof

2

REASON THROUGH ARGUMENTS

Charles, my youngest child, had a fondness for the Marvel superhero Iron Man and his alter-ego, Tony Stark. I did not know how much credibility he attributed to the comic book character until after watching the Avengers movie. In the movie, Thor hit Iron Man with a super bolt of lightning. This gave him enough energy to hit the God of Thunder back with "400% capacity" of the Iron Man suit. 400%? As an electronics engineer, I thought this was ridiculous. "Charlie," I said, "400% power capacity would have fried those circuits and melted his suit to a crisp."

My little boy looked at me with incredulity. "Mom, Tony Stark said so. It must be true!"

I told my husband about this exchange, saying, "My son believes a fictional character more than me!" My husband, a mechanical engineer, calmly replied, "Like somebody who didn't believe me when I said her car couldn't run on ethanol without undergoing conversion, just because her favorite Hollywood star said it could. Remember how that turned out?"

Touché, I thought. Robert Downey Jr.'s script claiming a technical impossibility is as reliable as a celluloid celebrity's advocacy concerning my car's appropriate fuel. The similarity in our thinking boils down to the same argument.

- First premise: Everything A says is true.
- Second premise: A made a statement.
- Conclusion: The statement must be true.

The argument would make sense assuming both premises were true. It is a valid argument. But the first premise turned out to be false. Thus, the reasoning was not sound, and the conclusion was false, too.

Reasoning And Argumentation

Arguments aim to convince or persuade. An argument lays down a claim and supports it with reasons. We also discussed reasoning as something all people do and logical reasoning, which not all people do. Logical reasoning is a systematic process. The structured expression of logical reasoning is what is called argumentation. Scholars often refer to arguments as "the language of logic."

Reasoning is different from argumentation; the first is the thought process, the second is how the thought process is expressed under logical principles. Argumentation expresses in a structured set of statements the reasons supporting a claim. Arguments have two elements: one or more premises and a conclusion.

All arguments include reasoning, but not all reasoning is argumentative. Some reasons are merely informative. Reasons intended for argumentation are those that aim to strengthen or weaken the acceptability of a certain claim. The probative goal is what distinguishes an argument from other forms of statements [1].

For an argument to be convincing, it is not enough for the conclusions and premises to be true. The premises should also provide compelling reasons to accept the conclusion. The grounds provided by the premises should be well-connected to the conclusion. How the argument lays out its premises and conclusion traces the logical reasoning that our minds journey through.

- A man's home is his castle. (True)
- The king lives in a castle. (True)
- The king is a man. (True)

In the above example, there are two premises and a conclusion. The premises are true, as well as the conclusion, and there is nothing inherently wrong with each statement. However, the premises do not convincingly lead to the conclusion – the conclusion stands as true even without the premises. The argument is not compelling because it fails to make a strong logical link between the premises and the conclusion.

Validity And Soundness

The validity of an argument is completely determined only by its structure, not its content. An argument may be valid even if it is not sound. An argument is valid if it takes a form that makes it impossible for the premises to be true, but the conclusion is false. Take the following argument:

- People born in 1990 are called millennials. (true)
- George Washington was born in 1990. (false)
- Therefore, George Washington is a millennial. (false)

If the preceding false premise is corrected and the structure is maintained, we have:

- People born in 1990 are called millennials. (true)
- Emma Watson was born in 1990. (true)
- Therefore, Emma Watson is a millennial. (true)

It is possible for a valid argument to have a false conclusion as long as at least one premise is false [2].

The distinction between validity and soundness can be complicated but intriguing. Let's go through them with some examples.

(1)In a valid argument, when all the premises are true, the conclusion is always true.

- All cats are mammals. (true)
- Lions are cats. (true)
- Therefore, lions are mammals. (true)

(2)Even if a premise is false, the conclusion can still be true and the argument is valid but unsound.

- Whales live in the ocean. (true)
- Hammerhead sharks are whales. (false)
- Therefore, hammerhead sharks live in the ocean. (true)

To test this argument's validity, let us change the second premise to make it true while retaining the argument's structure. So, it becomes:

- Whales live in the ocean. (true)
- Dolphins are whales. (true)
- Therefore, dolphins live in the ocean. (true)

Following the same structure, another argument with true premises can be:

- Professional ballet dancers are graceful and poised. (true)
- Olga Smirnova is a professional ballet dancer. (true)

- Olga Smirnova is graceful and poised. (true)

This is, therefore, a valid and sound argument.

(3)Likewise, even when both premises are true, the conclusion can still be false, leading to an invalid argument.

- Surfing is popular with tourists in Australia. (true)
- The Koala bear is popular with tourists in Australia. (true)
- The Koala bear is surfing. (false)

Notice that unlike the example in (2) above, the pattern is at fault in the last argument, not only the reasoning. Therefore, it is an invalid as well as unsound argument.

As previously shown in the example in (2), a valid argument can also have a true conclusion even if one premise is false.

The important thing to remember is that when the premises are true, and the reasoning is correct, the conclusion is true, and the argument is sound and valid.

There is another distinction between arguments, and these are the simple and the complex. Simple arguments have one or more premises and a conclusion. The earlier examples are all simple arguments.

On the other hand, a complex argument has a set of arguments whose premises and/or conclusions overlap.

Complex arguments have several intermediate conclusions and one final conclusion. Consider the following argument:

- Our survey showed that the proposed product is viewed positively by the market, so it enjoys high demand. However, the technology needed to produce it is experimental, which will be too costly to produce. The product must have a high demand and low cost to be adopted. Otherwise, it shall undergo further development.

The argument is difficult to analyze in its original form, so we break it down into its basic form, where **P** stands for the premise, **IC** for the intermediate conclusion, and **FC** for final conclusion.

- Pa1: The product scored positive market views.
- Pa2: Positive market views indicate high demand.
- ICa: The product has a high demand.
- Pb1: The technology needed is experimental.
- Pb2: Experimental technology is too costly.
- ICb: The technology needed is too costly.
- Pc1: The product has high demand but high cost.
- Pc2: The product must have high demand and low cost to be adopted.
- ICc: The product cannot be adopted
- Pd: If the product cannot be adopted, it will be further developed.

- FC: The product will be further developed.

We more frequently encounter complex arguments than simple arguments. Discussions or debates are complicated by many related issues that often require extended reasoning [3].

Deduction And Induction

There are two types of reasoning, deductive and inductive. Deductive reasoning is a fundamental form of logical inference that begins with a general theory narrowed down by information and reasoning to reach a specific conclusion. The scientific method uses this type of reasoning; it begins with a hypothesis, qualifies it with observations, and ends with a logical proof of the initial hypothesis [4]. "All planets in the solar system revolve around the sun. The Earth is a planet in the solar system. Therefore, the Earth revolves around the sun."

Inductive reasoning proceeds in the reverse direction. It begins with the specific observations and infers a general conclusion from them. Inductive reasoning requires a larger amount of empirical data than deductive reasoning. Patterns of relationships emerge from these data, and a general theory is formulated [5].

Inductive reasoning more often employs statistical probabilities. "I took out one candy from a pack of Skittles and found out it was red. I took out four candies more from the same pack, and they all turned out red.

Therefore, it is likely that my pack of Skittles contains all red candies."

There are two types of arguments that correspond to the types of reasoning. These are deductive and inductive arguments. The premises in the deductive form provide a conclusive proof of the claim. In the inductive form, the premises express the likelihood, but not the certainty, of the conclusion. Compare the following arguments:

Deductive argument:

- Left-handed people write better with their left hand.
- Arnold is left-handed.
- Arnold writes better with his left hand.

Inductive argument:

- Many left-handed people use left-handed scissors.
- Arnold is left-handed.
- Arnold uses left-handed scissors.

The difference between a deductive and inductive argument lies in the intention of the arguer [6]. In deductive arguments, the arguer guarantees that the conclusion is true by giving true premises. In inductive arguments, the arguer believes that the truth of the promises only gives good reason to believe that the conclusion is probably (but not definitely) true.

In the case of valid deductive arguments, the conclusion will always be true if all the premises are true. But in the case of inductive arguments, it is possible to have sound reasoning and still be wrong. This is because there is some doubt as to whether at least one of the premises is true.

Another difference between the two is that deductive arguments assert the claim that the truth of its premises guarantees the truth of its conclusion. If all the premises are true, then the conclusion must be true. In contrast, an inductive argument allows for some probability that the conclusion may be more likely true than not true, without guarantee either way.

Deductive arguments are either valid or invalid. The same terms cannot refer to inductive arguments; instead, they are either strong or weak [7]. Strong inductive arguments, like valid deductive arguments, do not need to have all true premises. Still, if both premises are true, then it is likely that the conclusion has a strong probability of being true. Cogency for inductive arguments is similar to soundness for deductive arguments, where both premises are true. All weak inductive arguments are uncogent, just as all invalid deductive arguments are unsound.

The terms used to describe deductive and inductive arguments are broken down and compared in the following diagram.

Argument Terminology

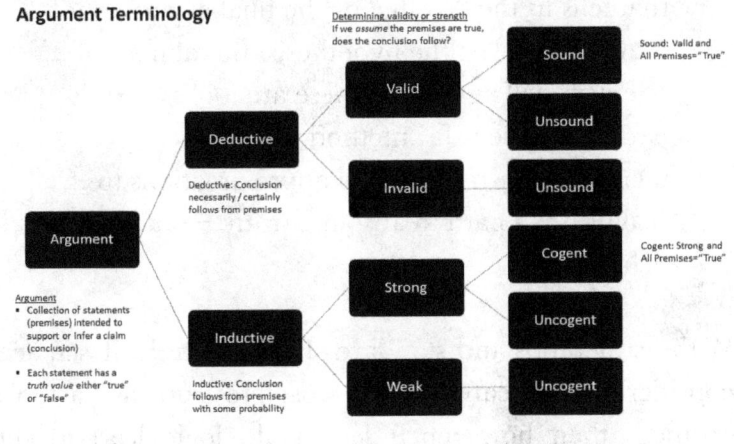

Source Information: Patrick J. Hurley "A Concise Introduction to Logic-12th Ed."

Source: DeMichele, T. (2017) [8]

Why We Argue

Why are we drawn to quarreling or trying to win an argument rather than seeking the truth? The question admits of many conflicting issues. The first is the elusive nature of truth. If truth were absolute, then it would be readily perceived and accepted. Then there would be little need for debate. If an absolute truth exists, it is one that observations can scientifically prove through the five senses. But there lies the crux of all problems — there is no simple answer, as there is no simple truth.

- [C]ollectively, we keep acting as though there are simple answers. We continually read about the search for the one method that will allow us to cut through the confusion, the one piece of data that tells us the "truth," or the final experiment that will "prove" the hypothesis. But almost all scientists will agree that these are fool's errands —that science is [a] method for producing incrementally more useful approximations to reality, not a path to absolute truth. – Gavin Schmidt [9]

With its methods and standards for exactitude, if science, considering the search for an absolute truth as "a fool's errand," then how much less could logic lead to the discovery of "the truth"? The search for the truth is one long, sustained debate. Even with the best of intentions, "seeking the truth" leads to many false paths. The only way to test these theories is to subject it to the crucible of debate, the tool of which is by winning the argument.

But bona fide intentions are not always assured. Often the goal becomes to win the argument at the expense of the truth because the truth is anyway relative. Cohen [10] of the New York Times sees this as the "need to triumph in the debating arena." The compulsion to decimate the opponent replaces the quest to seek the truth.

The Argumentative Theory of Reasoning, a theory developed by French cognitive social scientists to explain how rationality becomes a weapon. Mercier and Sperber [11]theorize that humans are dependent on communication and vulnerable to misinformation. "Skilled arguers are not after the truth but after arguments supporting their views" (p.57). Thus reasoning resorts to distorting facts and enabling mistaken beliefs to persist with winning as the motivation.

The same uncertainties about the truth underlie why we make guesses in place of observations. Observations are perceptions of the environment gathered by our five senses. We all observe the same things, but the mental interpretations of what we perceive differ depending on our age, experience, education, cultural and social orientation, and a host of other factors. Making an educated guess is part of our sense-making impulse. Our logic drives us to hypothesize in a manner that makes sense of our world in the face of new stimuli. Guessing is part of our normal logical process, and it is not wrong if it seeks subsequent validation through facts.

Action Steps

To better understand what an argument is, let us conduct a quick exercise formulated by Prof. Bradley H. Dowden of California State University [12]. Of the following four passages, identify which contains an argument based on its technical definition. Try to think about the exercise and exert some honest effort in arriving at an answer before checking out the solution that follows.

a. I hate you. Get out of here!

b. I'm sure Martin Luther King, Jr. didn't die during the 1960s because it says right here in the encyclopedia that he was assassinated in Memphis in 1998.

c. The Republican Party began back in the 1950s as a U.S. political party. Abraham Lincoln was their first candidate to win the presidency.

d. I don't believe you when you say Martin Luther King Jr. could have been elected president if he hadn't been assassinated.

What selection contains an argument, and what type of argument is it? (Try to exert your best effort to answer before proceeding to the solution at the end of the chapter.)

Moving On

Our children may swear allegiance to their superheroes, but their parents have no excuse to lapse into poor reasoning habits. Structuring our thinking along the lines of an argument clarifies the premises and their logical link to the conclusion we want to advance. It helps weed out the logical errors we often make, such as those we shall discuss in the next chapter.

Key Takeaways

- Reasoning is a thought process, while argumentation is organizing thoughts in a logical structure.
- A valid argument complies with the logical structure.

- Invalid arguments may be sound or unsound.
  Invalid arguments are always unsound.
- Arguments may be deductive or inductive.

Solution To The Activity:

Selection (a) is an argument in its common usage, but not in the logical sense. Selection (c) is a simple description of the Republican Party, without a logical relation between the two statements. Selection (d) is a mere statement of a belief. In (b), there is only one premise, and although arguments usually have two or more premises, one alone is acceptable [13].

The answer to the exercise is (b). Many of us would not have identified this as an argument because it alleges a falsity, i.e., that Martin Luther King was assassinated in 1998. However, even if an argument contains some bad information, it is nevertheless still an argument as long as there is a reason (a premise) and a conclusion that is logically related to the reason. In this case. The argument is a valid unsound deductive argument. In its classic form, it would be:

Martin Luther King was assassinated in 1998. (false)

The year 1998 is not in the 1960s. (true)

Therefore, Martin Luther King did not die in the 1960s. (false)

3

THE CULPRIT OF BAD REASONING: OUR LOGICAL ERRORS AND BIASES

> *She wore tight corsets to give her a teeny waist - I helped her lace them up - but they had the effect of causing her to faint. Mom called it the vapors and said it was a sign of her high breeding and delicate nature. I thought it was a sign that the corset made it hard to breathe.*[1]
>
> —Jeannette Walls, Half Broke Horses (2009)

I f there ever were a symbol of torture in the name of beauty, it would be the corset. Not only during the Victorian period but in any period in history. Why any woman would go to such suffering to appear to have a whistle bait waist just does not seem logical, justifying Walls' common-sense observation in that selection. But in her mother's eyes, it's more than just a ploy to get men's admiring attention. Corsets, to her mind, were a sign of noble pedigree and social stature.

Walls and her mother exhibited different biases toward a lady's undergarment that symbolized both privilege and pathos, depending on their perspective.

Bias, Stereotyping, Prejudice, And Discrimination

Psychologists draw a fine distinction among four words we use interchangeably: bias, stereotyping, prejudice, and discrimination. These elements are the cause of logical errors we make almost daily [2].

Stereotyping involves generalizing a characteristic over an entire group of people: "Canadians are polite while New Yorkers are rude." Employers who subscribe to this stereotype may give unfair attention to their employees' nationality or residency; this is called bias. When bias creates a positive attitude towards Canadians and a negative attitude towards New Yorkers, it becomes prejudice. Finally, if the employer hires Canadians over New Yorkers based on that prejudice, then the act is called discrimination.

Bias in a person's attitude leads to prejudice, which comes from the root words "pre" (before) and "judge" (decide). To prejudge is to render a conclusion before proper reasoning. It shortcuts reason and jumps to an assumption, a prejudgment, and therefore a wrong conclusion. In an argument, introducing a bias in the premises results in an error in the conclusion. An unsound argument, or a fallacy, is therefore created.

By its nature, a fallacy is not a moral thing, but the extent to which it may be good or evil depends upon the purpose it serves.

For instance, the police may use fallacies to convince a criminal to reveal facts he may know about a crime. "The superintendent may lighten your sentence if you reveal where the stolen goods are." This is a fallacy to the extent that the superintendent may not have the power to lighten the criminal's sentence. If it leads the criminal to reveal where a crime's evidence is, then the fallacy has been used for good.

However, the fallacy is bad if it intends to lead to a false outcome. "The superintendent will charge your son for conspiracy if you do not plead guilty." The fallacy here is that charges against the son will proceed unless the father pleads guilty, which amounts to coercion.

The key to good judgment, therefore, is to distinguish a fallacy from a sound argument. Not all fallacies have serious consequences; some are so commonplace that we encounter them daily. Parents may think that their daughter is more intelligent than their son because she gets higher math grades than him. This is fallacious because there are many kinds of intelligence. The son may be better at sports. Thus, he may have a higher bodily-kinesthetic intelligence while his sister has a higher logical-mathematical intelligence. They are thus equally intelligent in different ways.

Fallacies show a logical argument's deficiency because a logical connection between the premises and the conclusion remains unrevealed. The parents who mistakenly conclude that one child is more intelligent than the other are not aware that other measures determine intelligence. The suspect was not aware of the limitations in the superintendent's powers to lighten his sentence or charge his son without evidence. The premises stating these specific concerns are not present. Therefore, the parents and the suspect arrived at conclusions based on incomplete arguments.

It is difficult to detect a fallacy in real-world situations because cultural stereotypes, cultural biases, and past experiences tend to trick our minds into making irrelevant or invalid assumptions. The assumption fills the missing premise, the incomplete argument appears whole, and the invalid conclusion appears valid.

Action Steps

There are many methods of detecting formal fallacies. Three basic steps could quickly identify the type of common fallacy that tricks our minds into jumping to the wrong conclusion [3].

(1) Identify the wrong premises (the "bad proofs"). These can be outright misstatements or implied comparisons, or examples that are irrelevant to the conclusion. Celebrity brandings are a common type of fallacy. "Rihanna uses the Fenty Beauty brand of makeup. If I use it, I will look

as beautiful as her," implies a false comparison between the consumer and the celebrity. The omitted premise is "I am not Rihanna," therefore, what is good for Rihanna is not necessarily good for me.

(2) <u>Identify the wrong alternative outcomes</u>. The often-implied choices may not be the only ones possible, and awareness of other alternatives may prevent us from making the wrong decision. "Robert is handsome and rich, but he's a playboy. Tommy doesn't have a bad record, but he doesn't have a job either. Whom should I marry?" The answer does not have to be Robert or Tommy because it can be "neither one."

(3) <u>Identify logical disconnects between premises and conclusion</u>. Even if the proofs or evidence are true, they may not be entirely relevant to the conclusion or issue. "My parents died before the age of 65, and I have the same health conditions as they did. Therefore, I will also die before I reach 65 years." While it may be true that your parents died in middle age, and you may indeed have inherited their health problems, there is no logical certainty linking these premises and the certainty of your death. You may be living a healthier lifestyle, and the causes of their passing may not be due exclusively to your shared health conditions.

Moving On

Some people may think of a corset as a beauty aid; others see it as an Iron Maiden Lite. Having different frames of mind is unavoidable. People have biases that manifest as logical errors when least expected. Logical errors are fallacies, which we will learn more about in the next chapter.

Key takeaways

- Logical errors are rooted in personal biases.
- Biases in the premises of an argument result in unsound arguments or fallacies.
- Fallacies interfere in the logical connection between premises and conclusions.
- Finding fallacies involves identifying the false premise, the erroneous conclusion, or the logical disconnection between the premise and conclusion.

4

DEMYSTIFYING THE SO-CALLED FORMAL LOGICAL ERRORS

> *By and large, the truth is not merely a fierce battle with ignorance and fallacy, but, first and foremost, a combat with our own preconceived ideas and aprioristic conceptions.*[1]
>
> — ERIK PEVERNAGIE, LIFE QUOTES AND PAINTINGS (2007)

W hat is the truth? This is the question at the center of all philosophical inquiry, and there is no easy answer. We craft the way we see the world, and it is only through the rules of logic that we pierce through our misconceptions to perceive what truth is.

Our minds often interpret our surroundings through heuristics − rules of thumb, an educated guess, or trial-and-error − that shortcut the logical process. These result in recurring errors in reasoning we call fallacies. They are of five basic types.

1. Affirming The Consequent (*Modus Ponens*)

This error in reasoning is a logical fallacy known as affirming the consequent. Based on the result or consequent, the most readily apparent cause is assumed to be true without considering other possible causes [2]. It is of the form: "If P, then Q. Q. Therefore, P."

- If you were careless in driving, then the car would be dented.
- The car is dented.
- Therefore, you were careless in driving.

Many husbands and wives have quarreled over this argument. The fallacy lies in drawing a definite conclusion about the cause from the effect. When several causes are possible, our mind often focuses on the most obvious when some other explanation is possible. The dented car may have been struck by a moving object, such as another car, without the fault of the driver accused of carelessness.

- If John throws a ball in the house, then a window gets broken.
- A window is broken.
- Therefore, John threw a ball in the house.

The broker window could have resulted from many things other than John throwing a ball. The handyman could have miscalculated and swung a ladder into the window. Or it is also likely that Jill was the thrower and not John. Children, workers, or other subordinate persons often get unfairly blamed for mishaps, only to be later proven innocent to the chagrin of the accuser.

Could there be exceptions to the rule that the pattern redounds to a fallacy? What if the consequent can have only one cause?

- If there is a deadly build-up of toxic gas in the mine, it will kill the canary.
- The canary died.
- Therefore, there is a build-up of toxic gas in the mine.

From 1911 to 1986, miners used canaries in coal mines to detect carbon monoxide and other noxious gases. Strictly speaking, the canary can die of many other causes such as age or illness. It would have made sense, though, for the miners to bring young, healthy canaries with them to reduce the probability of other causes. Happily, for canaries, digital detectors replaced them in 1985 [3]. Their case shows that where a consequence can only result from one cause, affirming the consequent ceases to be a fallacy.

2. Denying The Antecedent (*Modus Tollens*)

This fallacy is also known as the fallacy of the inverse, or inverse error. Denying the antecedent is a formal fallacy wherein the inverse from the original statement is inferred. This is invalid because denying the antecedent does not necessarily imply denying the consequent [4]. Its form is: "If P, then Q. If not P, then not Q."

- If Mario is a professional golfer, then he is a good sportsman.
- But Mario is not a professional golfer.
- Therefore, he is not a good sportsman.

This argument's error is concluding that Mario is not a good sportsman solely because he is not a professional golfer. Not all good sportsmen are professionals since some engage in sports as a hobby, not a career. Mario may not even be good at golf, but he may be good at other sports – tennis, boxing, video sports – making him a good sportsman.

- If you take a teaspoon of virgin coconut oil every day, then you will remain healthy.
- You do not take virgin coconut oil.
- Then you will not remain healthy.

Staying healthy can result from many things, such as healthy exercise, sufficient rest, and having a healthy diet.

While virgin coconut oil can contribute to one's health, not taking it does not necessarily become unhealthy.

Again, be careful in determining whether or not ruling out the antecedent really does result in ruling out the consequent. Take the following example.

- If Zoe graduates from high school this year, then she could go to college next year.
- Zoe did not graduate from high school this year.
- Therefore, Zoe cannot go to college next year.

While this argument follows the pattern for modus tollens, the antecedent (graduating from high school) is a necessary requisite for the consequent (studying in college the following year). Lack of a high school diploma will not qualify Zoe for entrance into college.

3. Affirming A Disjunct

Another name of this fallacy is the false exclusionary disjunct. A disjunct refers to one of the terms of a disjunctive proposition that excludes one term from another. The fallacy of affirming a disjunct involved affirming one of two things disjoined, then denying the other term. The error is assuming that since one disjunct is false, the other should be true. The word OR is inclusive, allowing for one or both of the disjuncts to be true [5]. This fallacy has the form: "A or B. A. Therefore, not B."

- To get a scholarship, one should be either bright or good in sports.
- Andrew got a sports scholarship.
- Therefore, Andrew is not bright.

The first premise enumerates two ways of getting a scholarship. Andrew was good at sports, and so he earned a sports scholarship. While it was true that he did not earn an academic scholarship, this does not mean he was not bright. Being good in sports does not exclude being bright.

- Celia would love either a puppy or a kitten.
- Celia loved the puppy she got.
- That means she would not love a kitten.

Implicit in this example is the affection Celia has for animals in general and that she would love a puppy or a kitten, whichever she received. Celia received a puppy which she loved dearly. However, it is not right to say that she would not love a kitten if she received it – or both pets if she received both.

The disjunction is an "either-or" statement that implies the need for a choice. However, there are two types of disjunctions. The inclusive or weak disjunction allows for choosing one or both (either/or) of the alternatives. The exclusive or strong disjunction allows a single choice, and the selection of one alternative necessarily excludes the other.

- In the movie, Chris will play either Thor or Loki.
- Chris will play Thor.
- Therefore, Chris will not play Loki.

An exclusive or strong disjunction does not produce a fallacy under affirming a disjunct, because in this case, the affirming one disjunct denies the other. Whether a disjunction is inclusive or exclusive is implied by the nature of the disjunctive situation. Celia can love two pets, but Chris cannot play two major roles in the same movie (assuming it is a conventional movie and not employing digital special effects).

4. Denying A Conjunct

If a disjunct is a term disjoined from another, then a conjunct is a term joined to another as being in the same class. The fallacy consists of declaring, in the second premise, that one of the conjuncts is false, then concluding the other is true. The error lies in assuming that negating one of the conjuncts necessarily affirms the other when it is logically possible to negate both [6]. There are two forms for this fallacy

- Form 1: Not both p and q. Not p. Therefore q.
- Form 2: Not both p and q. Not q. Therefore, p.

An example for this fallacy is:

- Anthony is not both Catholic and atheist.

- Anthony is not Catholic.
- Therefore, he is an atheist.

Indeed, Catholics (a group of people who believe in God) are not atheists (people who do not believe in God), and vice-versa. But there are other groups who are not Catholic and still believe in God, so they are not atheists. Anthony could be a member of another Christian denomination or a Buddhist, Muslim, or Hindu. He may believe in God but be unaffiliated. There are alternatives other than being atheist.

- In the tournament, members of the same family cannot join both the basketball and football games.
- The Joneses did not join the basketball games.
- Therefore, the Joneses will join the football games.

This argument's fallaciousness lies in the possibility that the Joneses need not choose from the two contests. They may join another game, or even no game at all. The conjunction does not exclude this possibility.

By way of contrast, the validating forms for this conjunctive argument cure the logical error and dispel the fallacy. They are of the alternative forms (AF):

- AF 1: Not both p and q. P. Therefore, not q.
- AF 2: Not both p and q. Q. Therefore, not p.

So, the validating form for our conjunctive arguments would be:

- Anthony is not both Catholic and atheist.
- Anthony is a Catholic.
- Therefore, he is not an atheist.

- In the tournament, members of the same family cannot join both the basketball and football games.
- The Joneses joined the basketball game.
- Therefore, the Joneses will not join the football game.

The conjunctive argument and denying a conjunct have similar forms, so they are often confused for each other. Their difference lies in the second premise, which is negative in denying a conjunct and affirmative in the conjunctive argument. Denying a conjunct is fallacious and therefore not valid, while the conjunctive argument is valid and therefore not fallacious.

5. The Fallacy Of The Undistributed Middle (*Non Distributio Medii*)

This fallacy is a syllogistic fallacy because it is the form of a categorical syllogism.

- All A is B.
- All B is C.

- Therefore, all A is C.

The structure has two distinct but related premises, followed by a conclusion that embodies the deductive argument. The middle term is that term included in both syllogisms. Note that the basic syllogistic structure comprises a valid argument because as long as its prepositions are true, then it is logically sound.

When the use of the middle term in the argument includes all the members of that class, then the middle term is said to be distributed. If the term refers to only some of the members of the class, then it is undistributed. The rule of logic requires that the middle term should be distributed in at least one of the two premises for the syllogism to hold [7].

The fallacy of the undistributed middle is where the middle term (the common term in both premises) is not distributed in either premise. It has the form: "All Z is B. All Y is B. Therefore, all Y is Z." B, the middle term, is undistributed in both premises. The following is an example of this form of fallacy.

- All insects are animals.
- All mammals are animals.
- Therefore, all mammals are insects.

The middle term, animals, includes both insects and mammals as well as many other groups. The logical error is obvious: insects and mammals are different categories that exclude each other, even if they are both animals.

- All vampires are bloodsuckers.
- All female mosquitoes are bloodsuckers.
- Therefore, all vampires are female mosquitoes.

The absurdity of Count Dracula transforming into an annoying egg-laying insect rather than a bat highlights the fallacy of this statement.

A real-world scenario where the fallacy of the undistributed middle is logically invalid is in litigation [8]. A question arose in a legal case as to whether a "riverboat" must be registered as a "motorboat." The argument of the Bureau of Motor Vehicles was:

- Riverboats are watercraft.
- Motorboats are watercraft.
- Therefore, riverboats are motorboats and are subject to registration requirements.

The middle term in the syllogism is watercraft. The court ruled against this argument, and riverboats were adjudged exempt from registration.

Action Steps

Formal fallacies involve a weakness in the form or technical structure of an argument, rather than whether or not the conclusion is true. Five formal fallacies are listed below. Try to identify each of them. Make your best effort before finding the answers at the end of this chapter

1. All drivers are licensed, just as all physicians are licensed. That means all drivers are physicians!

2. If Elmer bought a new car, he would attract a lot of beautiful women. But he bought a used car, which is why women are not attracted to him.

3. Sally can play either the piano or the violin. She chose to play the piano, therefore she cannot play the violin.

4. You would lose the contest if you did not prepare well. You lost the contest, which only means that you did not prepare well.

5. My pet is not both a cat or a dog. My pet is not a cat. Therefore, it is a dog.

Moving On

Pevernagie calls the truth a battle within ourselves against our preconceived ideas. The truth is hard to accept, especially when it challenges our most precious convictions that are, nevertheless, wrong. Among our preconceived logical errors, formal errors are more readily found because they are signalled by faulty argument structures. Informal errors are more subtle and difficult to detect. We will learn about informal errors in the next chapter.

Key Takeaways

- Formal logical errors are faults in the structure of an argument.
- Affirming the consequent should not lead to affirming the antecedent.
- Denying the antecedent should not lead to denying the consequent.
- Affirming one disjunct should not deny the other disjunct.
- Denying one conjunct should not automatically affirm the other conjunct.
- The middle term should be distributed in one of the premises.

Solution To The Exercise:

1.Undistributed middle

2.Denying the antecedent

3.Affirming a disjunct

4.Affirming the consequent

5.Denying a conjunct.

THE INFORMAL LOGICAL ERRORS WE EXPERIENCE EVERYDAY

"**M**ommy, what is sex?"

Parents are bound to get this question from their children at some point, but I never thought I would hear it from my five-year-old son, Cedric, on the first day of kindergarten class. Making a mental note to accost his teacher when I had the chance, I sat Cedric on my knee, heaved a sigh, and launched the birds-and-the-bees talk meant for adolescents.

When I finished, he had a puzzled look. "O...K..." then he raised the card he was holding. "But how do I put all of that on this I.D.? The teacher said we should fill it up. I already put my name and age. But sex just has a small box. What should I write?"

"Oh. OH!... Just write 'M,' son!"

The little boy forgot about our talk just as quickly as he filled his card out, which is a relief. At times like these, I scold myself and promise to never repeat the same mistake. Yet, no matter how we might resolve to better discipline our minds, it is impossible to avoid the hundred-and-one lapses we make each day. It cannot be helped; our words crawl at a snail's pace while our ideas fly with eagles' wings.

Informal Fallacies

In Chapter 4, we encountered formal fallacies. They are the logical thinking errors that involve mistakes in the pattern of arguments and the relationships between premises and conclusions. However, some fallacies do not involve the formal structure but rather are logical errors we make everyday that involve unsound reasoning.

Informal fallacies are not limited to words and sentences but instead are more of logical misadventures. The logical mistakes that make up fallacies sometimes result from ill intent, inconsistency, irrelevance and insufficiency. More often, they emerge from simple misconceptions and force of habit. We frequently find ourselves committing mistakes in reasoning and judgment that turn out to be predictable because we have made them before.

Why Do We Tend To Make Predictable Logical Mistakes?

Funder [1] touches on the social nature of logical errors and why we tend to repeat them when faced with real-world situations even though we are already aware of them. In his seminal study, Funder distinguished "error" from "mistake," describing the error as an incorrect judgment of an experimental stimulus (i.e., a situation studied in isolation) and mistake as an incorrect judgment of a real-world stimulus.

We tend to treat errors as "shortcomings" of judgment, equivalent to the degree to which people can "reason well" or "make good decisions." It is a deviation from a model, an ideal, of how a judgment should be made. The mistake is done unintentionally.

- Every Black Friday, Sasha goes on an irrational buying binge. She fights for her place in line and rushes to grab the fast-moving merchandise, only to end up buying things she doesn't even need or want. Every year, Sasha resolves to avoid the next Black Friday rush, but every year finds her back.

Sasha knows that it defies reason to buy things she does not need just because they are on sale, but many people are like Sasha. She is caught up in the mad dash, doing what everybody else is doing but not really thinking. Commercial retailers exploit consumers' irrational buying impulses as part of their marketing strategy. Thus, a logical error becomes a recurring mistake driven by real-world conditions.

There are other reasons why we repeat the same logical errors. One is the degree to which we recall our past successes and failures, but recall does not improve the likelihood of not committing the error. People find it difficult to recall mistakes they have made because it is more difficult to remember many mistakes than just one or two. Trying to recall only makes the mental process slower and more deliberate and may lead to making even more mistakes [2].

Child: "Dad, may I go to Cecile's party?"

Dad: "Go ask your mother."

Child: "She said to ask you."

Dad: "Okay then, just be sure to get home on time."

And so the child leaves.

Mom: "Where's Bernadette?"

Dad: "She went to her classmate's party. I allowed her."

Mom: "Why? I didn't give my permission. I grounded her for not doing her homework."

Silence.

Mom: "She pulled a fast one on you again, huh?"

Dad: "I never learn."

Dad is not entirely at fault because his daughter could have asked his permission many times in the past to circumvent her mother. Sometimes it was right to give permission, and sometimes it was not. Trying to recall all those times his wife probably agreed with him and the other times she did not could make mental recall slower and more difficult.

Emotions also play a role in our judgment or decision-making process. How we feel shapes our decision-making process, such that logically correct decisions are avoided if they trigger negative feelings and vice-versa [3].

Ingrid: "I never learn. This is the fifth time I caught him with another girl. Every time he begs for forgiveness, saying he will change his ways. And every time I believe him."

Stella: "So this time you kicked him out?"

Ingrid: "I can't. What if this is the last time and he really changes?"

These theories about social contexts, emotions, and slow recall have broad application in our psychological make-up and give us some insight into how our minds work. It explains why we often commit the same logical mistakes as those we had already known to be errors.

Fallacies We Commonly Encounter

Ever heard of gremlins? Early English folklore described them as mischievous little creatures with spiky backs, large eyes, sharp teeth, and claws. They cause aircraft and other machines to malfunction in a way that mystifies mechanics. They appeared in the 1984 American movie [4], where the repugnant creatures popped out from a cute little fluffy pet called mogwai.

Everybody said, "How could such ugly monsters come from such a cute thing?"

Informal fallacies are much like gremlins. Disguised as sound reasons, they are actually naughty creatures that cause malfunctions in our thought processes. While our rational brain is off-guard, sneaky black swans, red herrings, straw men, slippery slopes, and a host of other well-concealed tricks and traps hijack our reasoning to create confusion and mischief. Before we know it, we end up with faulty conclusions and decisions that bring embarrassment and regret.

We are often unaware of the informal logical errors we make even as we are making them. They are mostly inadvertent, but sometimes we even resort to them intentionally to win an argument by confusing our opponent or to justify an unsound decision. Informal fallacies are more difficult to identify than formal fallacies because, unlike formal fallacies, the logical mistake does not reduce to a readily identifiable thought pattern.

There are more than a hundred informal logical errors, but we will discuss those most commonly encountered. Identifying them and understanding how they constitute unsound reasoning will help us avoid making erroneous decisions when we encounter them.

1. Hasty Generalization

A generalization is a statement about a group stating that all, some, or a proportion of the group's members, possess a particular attribute. A simple generalization could be, "Cows give milk." This is a commonly accepted truth, but it would have been more accurate to say, "Some cows give milk," because cows that do not become pregnant and give birth do not produce milk. The average milk-giving cycle for cows is three years [5]. Generalizations are the general rule, accepted as true despite some exceptions.

Hasty generalizations are fallacies of missing evidence. In this type of fallacy, the conclusion is arrived at based on insufficient or biased evidence, and therefore is not logically justified. Sometimes, the conclusion is based on vaguely-recalled anecdotes. It is also called "the fallacy of insufficient samples."

- The ocean voyage was marred by mishaps and unfortunate events, ever since the cook Damien joined them at the last port of call. They therefore suspected that Damien was the Jonah onboard.

Practically all sailors believe that their voyage over the perilous waters depends on luck due to the uncertainty of their journey. Superstitions catch on as a "general rule" even if there is little evidence to substantiate them. So rational decision-makers should set them aside, even if so-called anecdotal evidence seems particularly persuasive.

In quantified research, the conclusion may involve findings anchored on an unrepresentative or misspecified sample instead of a sample that is more aligned with the overall population.

- The findings of the study suggested that the student population of the university consisted of 80% women. Members of the survey sample came from three programs: nursing, women's and gender degrees, and elementary education.

If the researchers drew the samples from groups where one attribute (in this case, gender) is dominant, it does not necessarily introduce a problem IF the conclusion is attributed only to those groups. However, if results from a skewed sample are generalized over a wider population, then the conclusion is misleading. To obtain a reliable conclusion for the entire university in the situation above, the sample should include enrollees in engineering, military science, the seminary, or other programs where males may dominate, or programs where both genders are present to the same degree. The trick, of course, is to garner a sample sufficient to represent the target population.

A hasty generalization may also make a general conclusion out of a particular situation or a single piece of supporting evidence; this is "the fallacy of the lonely fact" [6].

- While the professor was proctoring an exam, the

college clerk came and spoke to him briefly at the classroom doorway. When he turned back to the class, he saw two students whispering and giggling. He presumed that the class took advantage of his brief distraction and cheated behind his back. He stopped the exam and gave the entire class a failing grade.

However, even if the sample size were large, the bias is obvious that it makes the conclusion unconvincing. Sometimes the conclusion is made over an entire group of people based on observations made over a few of their members. It may result in judgments that may seem unethical or even slanderous.

- A group of hikers were trekking across a hill considered sacred ground by the indigenous people. The site was so popular among tourists that the natives became wary of visitors to the area. When the hikers rested, one of them, unbeknownst to his companions, etched "U.S.A." on the trunk of a hundred-year-old tree. The native residents discovered the offending mark, and upon their petition the local government banned all American tourists from entering the area.

In this case, the act of one member of a group was taken to represent the act of all. The consequence of a single act was imposed upon all Americans because of the letters "U.S.A." etched on a tree. The situation becomes more absurd with the possibility that the offender might not even be from the U.S.A., which makes the generalization all the more irrational.

Addressing The Fallacy:

It is important not to rush to judgment. Begin by finding other data on the same issue, then weighing whether these are sufficient to overturn the generalization made.

2. Appeal To Authority

In reasoning, we try to find solid ground, outside of our own thinking, to anchor our premises. Whether they be persons, institutions, or classical texts, authorities are powerful sources of corroboration or contradiction of our assumptions. But reliance on the authority, if not properly established, can become a fallacy that traps the unwary.

In appeals to a person of authority, the argument is that something must be true because an alleged expert on the matter claimed it as true. This is also called an appeal to *false* authority.

- Will advised us to bring flowers when visiting our daughter's German mother-in-law for the first time. Will visited Germany once, and he was married and divorced five times, so he must know a lot about German mothers-in-law.

- Ramon always uses Axe Body Spray. If it is good enough for Ben Affleck, then it is good enough for Ramon.
- Madame Esperanza, the fortune teller, announced that the planets' alignment this year will bring either good fortune or bad luck, depending on your zodiac sign.

The three authorities in these examples are Will (not a German), Ben Affleck, the actor, and Madame Esperanza, the fortune teller. Obviously, their claims to authority are not strong. Will relies on stock knowledge, Ben Affleck is a paid endorser, and Madame Esperanza dabbles in mysteries that defy explanation and credulity. It is easy to see why they would be false authorities.

But what if Will's single visit to Germany was for ten years, Ben Affleck's global fan club members agree that he does smell nice, and Madame Esperanza is the national president of Psychics of America who happened to validate her predictions based on their knowledge of the mystic arts?

Suppose all sides agree that the person cited as an advocate is truly a reliable authority on the subject of discussion. In that case, this argument is not a fallacy for the parties concerned, but an inductive argument – i.e., an argument that is neither valid nor invalid, sound nor unsound.

It may be weak or strong, cogent or uncogent. Still, to the eyes and ears of their believers, it is an argument that admits of some probability because it comes from an authority they collectively recognize.

- According to the feng shui expert, it is bad luck to align the front door and the back door of a dwelling or business establishment without any obstruction between them. The flow of good energy that comes in the front door will quickly escape through the back door without first moving through the home or workplace.
- The Farmer' Almanac, which sells four million copies each year [7], stated that there would be sunny and cool weather from November 5 thru 10, but from February 12 to 19, there will be heavy snow in some places close to the eastern seaboard.

It is not a secret that all traditional Chinese individuals and establishments consult a feng shui expert before making major decisions. It is also undeniable that the Farmer's Almanac, established in 1792 [8], continues to provide online advice to all farmers and gardeners [9]. A subsequent section will discuss parallels between these types of arguments and appeals to faith.

There are two special cases of appeal to authority fallacies.

2.1 Citing An Authority Out-Of-Context

Decisions are better if one can rely on the actual words of a known authority. But at times, the message conveyed is wrong because the words are incomplete, out of context, or misrepresented.

Doctor: "Lina, you should cut down on carbohydrates."

Lina: "But Doc, you said I could have one cup of carbs per meal."

Doctor: "Uh, uh, listen, Lina. One cup of carbs per day." Monica's teacher told her class, "I won't give you written assignments this weekend, but when you go home, read the chapter because we will have a long examination on Monday." When Monica's mother asked, "Don't you have homework to do, Monica?" The youngster replied, "No, Mom. The teacher said we don't need to do homework this weekend."

Quoting or citing an authority out of context is done to make it appear that the authority is backing a position favorable to the arguer. In truth, the true position of the authority is neutral or opposite to the misrepresentation.

The fallacious statement is actually close to the authority's true statement and only differs slightly. Sometimes, the difference may be due to a misunderstanding (i.e., "per meal" is understood as "per day") or a lack of understanding (i.e., Monica does not have a written assignment, but she has a reading assignment).

Addressing the fallacy:

Often, we fail to discern a statement out of context just from the statement itself unless some background research is done on the authority supposedly making it.

If the authority is a celebrity, what were her past opinions on the matter, and are they consistent with the present alleged statement?

If we personally know the authority cited, the best is to ask if she really stated it as reported. Monica's mother could call the teacher or probably another parent to verify if what Monica said was true.

2.2 Appeal To Faith

When an argument bases its claim on faith, then take care in analyzing the argument. There are claims citing the authority of a written religious text of wide acceptance such as the Bible, Torah, or Koran, or a person such as the Pope, Mohammed, or minister of established reputation. In such instances, where all parties agree on the authority, it should not be regarded as a fallacy but as an inductive argument [10].

However, there are times when the authority relied upon is a belief, a norm handed down by tradition, or some other amorphous thing. The premise redounds to an accepted dogma or divine truth that defies proof. This can be tricky because, for believers, faith goes beyond logic or reason.

- The angel of God appeared to me and told me
  to establish a chapel at the mountaintop. If you
  have faith, you will see that I tell the truth.

The truth of the angel's appearance to the speaker is not
what makes this a fallacy, but his declaration that those
with faith will believe him. The reality is that some people
of faith will not believe in him because they may decide
that he lacked credibility. The claim seeks its validation in
faith, possibly because there is no other way to prove it.

However, we should beware that the mere mention of
faith or belief as the basis for a claim does not
immediately redound to a fallacy. The following are
instances when a faith-rationale was first dismissed as
fallacious and then subsequently validated by gaining
general acceptance and recognition.

- The fifth commandment says, "Thou shalt not
  kill." Therefore, even in a war, I will not hold a
  rifle or a knife to kill my enemy.

In World War II, Desmond Doss signed up with the U.S.
infantry as a conscientious objector – he would not hold a
rifle even during training. A devout Seventh-day Adventist
he believed that taking a life even in a war is against
God's will. For his stubbornness, he was frequently
ridiculed and reviled. Subsequently, he served as a medic
and served with distinction, saving the lives of more than
100 men. Soon after, he received the Medal of Honor for
his actions [11]. His extraordinary conviction became the

subject of a recent biographical motion picture, Hacksaw Ridge [12].

- The Hindu faith venerates rats as holy, and rodents have occupied a sacred place in Indian history. Rats should, therefore, never be exterminated.

Rodents are considered the source of disease and pestilence, for which modern-day sensibilities require their eradication. However, in India, they are venerated and have been for centuries, as seen in archaeological sites in that country [13]. To this day, the Temple of Rats stands in the State of Rajasthan in India to honor the Hindu deity Karni Mata.

- Islam considers charging interest for a loan as an unjust and immoral practice. Therefore, banks cannot condone interest payments.

Modern banking is founded on the concept of the time value of money and that the use of monies loaned out must earn interest. However, followers of Islam are forbidden by Shariah law to charge or pay Riba (interest) because this is an uncharitable and usurious practice [14]. This is irreconcilable with Western practice. However, with the rise of Islamic banking, interest-free banking products have been made available even through the traditional banking system.

- Thirteen is considered an unlucky number. That is why many high-rise buildings do not designate the 13th floor.

Originally, (and sometimes still) dismissed as superstitious with no basis in logic, there exists an aversion for the unlucky number 13. In the construction of high-rise buildings and particularly hotels, however, the tradition has caught on not to have a thirteenth floor, or if one existed, to not have it accessible by elevator. Building designers, construction companies, and elevator companies have, therefore, adopted the practice of not including the 13th floor if clients specify it. Hotel guests and building tenants refuse to stay or rent spaces on the thirteenth floor, thereby institutionalizing the practice [15].

Addressing The Fallacy:

Be cautious in immediately identifying faith- or belief-based reasons as fallacious. Suppose all parties involved agree that the value or belief is irrelevant, in that case, the argument reduces to a Red Herring (another fallacy), and the premise alleging the value becomes an irrelevant issue.

If some parties believe in the veracity of the value or belief, and others do not, then it would be foolish to debate what conflicting sides already consider undebatable. The most sensible recourse is mutual respect and to agree to disagree.

Why is it important to look into people's belief patterns when evaluating appeals to authority or faith? Human beings are complex creatures in whom logic and belief or faith play powerful roles in decision-making.

At all times, we should keep in mind that the decisions we make affect or involve other people, those with whom we may or may not share the same set of beliefs or values. This is particularly true in our current global business setting and international collaborations.

Therefore, when your Chinese business partner suggests that the new restaurant should face east because the feng shui expert said so, think twice before calling his reasoning irrelevant.

3. Appeal To Emotions

This fallacy is also known as manipulative appeals to pathos, manipulation of emotions, or "playing to the gallery." The "gallery" refers to the members of the general public who are naïve or gullible and who are easily swayed by emotional narratives. Arguments that play to the emotions are far from rational; people resort to when there are no good reasons to support the claim. Unsurprisingly, appeals to emotion comprise commercial advertisements.

- Fine dining restaurants and hotels advertise their Valentine's Day packages by showing a handsome couple apparently in love and

enjoying an elegant candle-lit dinner in one of
these establishments.

- Charities and foundations advertise for
  sponsorships and donations by highlighting the
  plight of poor families or the pitiful conditions of
  children in need.

There are specific types of emotions that a fallacy can
appeal to. There are five appeals to emotion frequently
used.

3.1 Appeal to Pity

- "Please include me in the graduation
  ceremonies, Dean Smith, please! My family is
  here, including my relatives from abroad,
  because they thought I had passed! And they're
  all dressed up! Would you break their hearts?"

Dean Smith should not allow an unworthy student to
graduate because this violates the rules. If he gives way to
pity, he acts with official authority and publicly conveys a
degree on an unworthy student, further compromising the
school.

3.2 Appeal To Fear

- Ordering online can be dangerous. Roy ordered

online using his credit card, and in two days, he found out that all his accounts were hacked! Better go and purchase the product personally so you can pay cash.

Ordering online can be safe with the proper precautions by using third-party payor services. There are advantages to making in-person purchases, but these are rational considerations that have nothing to do with the fear of credit fraud.

- Children, you'd better finish everything on your plate. When you die, your soul will come back to pick up every grain of rice you ever left behind.

Sometimes the fear inspired comes as a fateful consequence for defying the unwritten law. This is particularly effective in scaring children into following since they do not question the logical soundness of it.

3.3 Assigning Guilt by Association

- Members of the jury, the accused, is a Hong Kong national and may well be part of the 14-K Triad, the largest drug trafficking syndicate in the world whose roots also are in Hong Kong.

Not all Hong Kong nationals are Triad members, just as not all Mexicans are MS-13 members, and not all

Japanese are members of the Yakuza. Real guilt should attach because of real culpability, not imagined ones.

3.4 Appeal To Group Loyalty

- Juliet, as a member of the Alpha-Gamma-Phi sorority, you are forbidden from striking a friendship with Romeo because he belongs to the Sigma-Theta-Omega fraternity, our long-time adversaries.

Juliet is free to befriend Romeo if she wants to, except if she is a minor and there are real concerns to forbid her from such friendships (such as a rap sheet in Romeo's name). Group loyalty should not constrain discretion about one's personal affairs.

3.5 Appeal To Shame

- Alejandro, you are the son of the chief justice and the grandchild of the author of our nation's civil code. But you flunked your first year of law school! What will your father's colleagues think? His law fraternity?

Alejandro can tell his parents he's not interested in becoming a lawyer and instead pursues his passion for music and the arts.

The five arguments above can be quite convincing for people who decide based on their knee-jerk reactions when faced with problems. Deep emotional involvement in a dilemma can persuade one to decide in favor of quickly easing the personal discomfort he or she is facing, even if the decision is not well thought out.

Addressing The Fallacy:

Looking past the short-term reactions by thinking the problem through can prevent future regrets. When faced with an argument that triggers deep emotional reactions, the best is to refrain from deciding at the moment to provide time for calm and reflection.

Also, remember that fallacy notwithstanding, the claim may still be true if backed by reason, so keep an open mind. What is important is that the decision should not be solely based on emotion, without thinking of the long-term repercussions that may lead to regrets later. Decide based on logic rather than impulse

4. Appeal To Ignorance

Some arguments base their claim on the absence of any evidence that disproves it. When an argument reasons that something is either true or false based on a lack of evidence, this appeals to ignorance [16]. It is fallacious because a non-proof affirms nothing, therefore concluding that it affirms something is an absurdity.

Take the following frequently-encountered argument.

- Can anybody vouch for where you were on the night of the crime? If you do not have an alibi, then you are guilty.

In cop shows, too much emphasis is sometimes placed on the alibi of a suspect. If he cannot prove by objective testimony that he was somewhere else, the crime investigators regard him as guilty. But such is not the case, not even under the law enforcement procedures that movies try to imitate. We have been conditioned to believe that we may be found guilty of a crime because we may not have an alibi. Without positive proof beyond a reasonable doubt, one cannot be convicted based on mere suspicion.

- Your teacher suspects that you cheated in the last exam. Prove to us that you did not cheat, or you will be suspended.

It is impossible to prove a negative proposition. What you can do is prove the impossibility that you cheated – such as not having taken the test at all.

- There is no proof that intelligent life exists on other planets. Therefore, the earth is the only planet where there is intelligent life.

The absence of proof simply means that access to possible evidence is lacking. This is the same dilemma as the tree falling in the middle of a forest when there is nobody around to hear it. The fact that nobody was around to hear the crash does not mean there was no noise.

- There is no scientific proof of an afterlife.
  Therefore, there is no life after death.

Proof comes in many forms, depending on the orientation of the parties involved in the discussion. Scientific proof refers to the positivist approach that requires evidence observed by the five senses and analyzed through the scientific method. However, the interpretivist or constructivist approach allows for proof using observers' subjective interpretation or construction of their experiences. A conclusion arrived at through the use of one method of proof may not be the same conclusion reached by another method, therefore, it is important to consider how the listener interprets the evidence.

- DNA testing is not available in this remote country, so Sally cannot prove that John is the father of her child. Therefore, John is not the father of Sally's child.

This proof specifies one of several methods, although it is the most accurate and conclusive. However, the inability to carry out a DNA test is not justification for ruling out paternity nor. Neither is it, of course, the justification for ruling in its favor. The matter is simply inconclusive.

The appeal to ignorance works as a fallacy only if the absence of proof still admits that other possible conclusions may exist. The possibility of multiple outcomes is an important element of appeal to ignorance. But if the possibilities are finite and all are ruled out except one, then the remaining possibility must be true. This is a case where the absence of proof is proof of the claim.

- Josie said she would be waiting for me at the Starbucks near her school. But there are two Starbucks stores near her school, one at 1st Street and the other at Main Street. Josie is not in the Main Street Starbucks, so she must be waiting for me at 1st. Street.

Josie has confirmed her presence at one of two places, and she is not present at one of them. Then it is conclusive that Josie is at the other place.

- The pea is under one of three shells. The shells at the left and the right are empty. Therefore, the pea is under the shell in the middle.

The shell game is a popular sleight-of-hand trick to fool people into thinking that an object can be only under one of three shells. The truth is the trick is played by the illusionist deftly concealing the pea in his or her hand rather than placing it under the shells. This makes the possibilities four instead of three, and the pea's absence in the two outer shells reduces the choice to two – under the middle shell or in hand. For certainty to prevail in an appeal to ignorance exception, there must be good faith and full disclosure of all the alternative possibilities. Otherwise, the fallacy holds.

- There are only four men on this island, but Paul, George, and Ringo are all infertile. Therefore, John is the father of Sally's child!

Implicit in this example is that Sally has not left the island. Therefore, only four men could have fathered her child. By ruling out the three, one can safely conclude that John is the father even without a DNA test.

- If there is no evidence proving his guilt, then he must be declared innocent.

In logic, the absence of evidence that a suspect committed the crime does not prove guilt or innocence. However, the presumption of innocence is mandatory by operation of law. It is a legal convention that ensures a person is not put in a position of uncertainty; therefore, he is either innocent or guilty based on the availability of evidence.

- The crime alleged is armed insurrection. But

there is no proof that the people were armed.
Therefore, there is no crime.

The presumption of innocence under the law is conclusive unless evidence arises to the contrary. In criminal law, the necessary elements of the crime are identified, and the burden of proof is placed on the party making the allegation. If the evidence fails to prove all the necessary elements of the crime, then it is as if there is no evidence, and the accused is presumed innocent of the crime charged.

Addressing The Fallacy

Before declaring that an appeal to ignorance is fallacious, we should ensure that the absence of proof exhausts all other possibilities or that a legal presumption does not exist that dictates the conclusion when evidence is not present. If alternatives are possible other than the claim the argument makes, we need not fall for arguments based on the absence of proof.

5. Black Swan Fallacy

This is a fallacy arising from the tendency of people to ignore evidence that runs counter to their presumptions and beliefs. Its name derives from the generally held belief that all swans are white, therefore, if a bird is a swan, then that bird must be white. That general belief proved false, however. A Dutch explorer named Willem de Vlamingh chanced upon black swans in Australia during a rescue mission, for which reason the black swan was incorporated in the flag of Western Australia [17]. His discovery also disproved the presumption that all swans are white.

There is a presumption that everyone takes to be true in a black swan fallacy, but that turns out later to be false. This presumption was the basis for a decision that the arguer thinks he or she is making with certainty because of the certainty of the presumption (i.e., the white swan). Overturning the presumption, therefore, also overturns the soundness of the conclusion.

- Tropical countries do not have winters.
- Winters are needed to train athletes in winter sports.
- Tropical countries could not train athletes in winter sports.

Most people would presume that countries in tropical regions are unable to compete in winter games because of their balmy climate. In 1992, the first ice skating rink in Asia was built in the Philippines. In 2014, Michael Martinez became the first skater who grew up and trained in Southeast Asia to qualify for the Winter Olympics. The fallacy, therefore, lies in the presumption that countries without winters could not train local athletes to compete in any winter sports.

- Our Australian trip was scheduled for July, so I brought all my summer clothes, swimwear, tanning lotion, and beach towels. Wrong decision: Winter in Australia spans June to August.

The argument mentions July, which, in the U.S., is summertime. Some American might presume the seasons are the same in another country without realizing that they are actually reversed for southern-hemisphere states

The arguments above deal with the common erroneous mental images that many people have about people or things. The mistaken associations are due more to a mindset brought by common usage rather than prejudice.

The Black Swan fallacy can also refer to the belief that something a person has never witnessed cannot exist. Philosophers point to the Black Swan discovery as a metaphor for discovering that something a person thought impossible is possible [18].

Take the two following real-life stories about things thought to be impossible turning out to be quite possible.

- Arnold's grandmother asked him if he wanted to go on a trip with them. She said, "If you decide to come, you will lose your birthday this year." Arnold thought it was impossible to lose his birthday, so he decided to join his grandparents on the trip. They left Los Angeles on January 9th and arrived in Manila on January 11th. They lost one day, January 10th, crossing the International Date Line – and that's how Arnold lost his birthday for that year.

- Juan courted Anita for six long years. In the seventh year, he asked her, "Anita, when will you agree to marry me?" Anita replied, "When the crow turns white," which is women-speak for "Never." But Juan would not be deterred. The next day, he gave Anita a computer printout of a crow with entirely white plumage. Apparently, 1% of the Corvus Brachyrhynchos, or American Crows, are afflicted with "albinism." Touched by his persistence (and because she always kept her promises), Anita married Juan before the year's end.

While these stories' outcomes were not seriously detrimental, so-called "impossible" conditions may be written into contracts.

- The co-parties agree to the finality of the merger in ten years unless a regime change takes place in Cambodia, where they will establish the joint venture.

A contracting party may feel confident that a coup d'etat has little to no chance of happening in ten years, only to be caught by it happening in the tenth year.

. . .

How could one avoid the pitfalls of the black swan fallacy? Nothing short of vigilance regarding the implications of words and phrases that stand out in the argument. By its very name, a "black swan" is something believed to be impossible because nobody has ever seen it [19]. Therefore, unless it is encountered then there is no way of knowing that it is possible.

The best way is to thoroughly research assertions, conditions, and stipulations that suggest a remote possibility. Where possible, rule out expressions that appear to be idiomatic or figurative (such as "unless the crow turns white"). Instead, couch the argument in plain language. When conditional language is necessary (as in a contract), anchor the conditions in known rather than unknown events. It will eliminate many future unwelcome surprises.

6. Begging The Question

This fallacy occurs when at least one of the premises of the argument assumes that the conclusion is true instead of reinforcing or proving it. In effect, the claim is assumed to be true even without proof. Another term for the fallacy is "Arguing in a Circle" [20].

The name "begging the question," which literally means "a question that begs to be answered," is perplexing because there is no question at all that begs to be answered. The fallacy assumes the conclusion and does not leave any doubt about it. It's Latin translation is petitio principii ("petitio" meaning petition, appeal to or beg, "principii" meaning the principle, or issue in question) [21]. The transition suggests that "begging the question" happened to be a direct translation of the Latin term, which did not really convey the essence of the fallacy.

Take the following examples of the circular fallacy.

- In the year 2000, the world will end as we know it, because at 12:01 a.m. on that day, all power will turn off, planes will fall from the sky, phone lines will go dead, and we will return to the Dark Ages.

The foregone conclusion in the argument above the sinister Y2K will definitely take place, and as proof, the premises list all the tragedies that will occur because of it. The premises do not explain the reasons or causes supporting the claim that a worldwide disaster will take place at the turn of the millennium. To set the argument straight, it could have explained that all computers upon which all automated information processing relies will reset to the double zero "00" due to faulty programming. It was a false analysis, but at least it cited a possible cause, not an effect, of Y2K.

- Golf is a popular sport because many people enjoy playing it.

Any sport gains popularity because it is loved and enjoyed by many people. It is the definition of "popular." Therefore, the premise of the above argument merely restates the conclusion. This is singular reasoning.

- The government should legalize cannabis for recreational purposes because many people find pleasure in indulging in its use.

The argument is a play on the word "recreational," which, in its legal sense, is the contrast of "medicinal" or used for therapeutic purposes. Arguing that cannabis should be accepted for recreation because many people enjoying it is a mere restatement of the nature of its use. A sound argument would explain why the law should eliminate recreational marijuana from the list of narcotics prohibited by law, such as the discovery that such use of the substance does not harm human health.

Begging the question does not require any question at all, differentiating it from the complex question fallacy. There are two questions involved in the latter, where the answer to a given question presumes an answer given to a previous question. There is no circular reasoning in this latter fallacy, but an implied answer to a hidden question.

- Inspector to suspect: "So when did you last beat up your wife?"

In this complex question, an affirmative answer to a hidden question, "Did you beat up your wife?" was presumed, without giving the suspect a chance to deny it. Actually, police interrogation tactics sometimes use this ploy to trick the suspect into a confession by making him believe that his crime has already been proven.

Addressing The Fallacy

It takes a quick mind to detect circular fallacies. Try to identify which in the argument is the evidence for the claim. If it is very similar to or something that the claim already includes, then you have a circular fallacy. Ask for more evidence, additional examples, or proof that chronologically precedes the claim. If the arguer can supply none, you know that there is no sound premise, and therefore the argument is fallacious.

7. Black-Or-White Fallacy

As the name implies, this fallacy forces a choice between only one or the other extreme choice (either black or white) when there are other alternatives (gray areas) to choose from. The fallacy is forcing a choice between only two alternatives.

A black or white fallacy is deceptive because it tricks the listeners into thinking that only two choices are possible, and the absence of merit in one makes acceptance of the other extreme the only solution. The arguer presents the quality that contrasts the two choices as the only important criterion for decision-making.

- Chloe's mother disapproved of her desire to enroll in a fine arts course. "Being an artist does not guarantee a good income. Better choose medicine as your career because doctors earn well!"

Many high school seniors who are about to select their college programs face this decision. Realistically, the choice does not have to be between Chloe's or her mom's. Chloe's interest is in the arts; her mom's interest is for her to have a well-paying career. Chloe could choose to meet both interests by enrolling in an advertising arts program. A career in the advertising arts is both artistically inclined and financially rewarding.

- Would you rather choose to marry for love or money?

This is a classic non-dilemma. Old movies frequently have the heroine choosing between a dashing, young indigent and a cold, aloof millionaire. In real life, one can choose to develop a caring, loving relationship with a person you can build a comfortable life.

- When investing in a restaurant business, it is better to put up a fine-dining restaurant rather than a fast-food outlet.

Making business decisions requires an open and creative mind. There are numerous business models in this industry other than fine-dining and fast-food, such as bistros, buffets, diners, etc. Innovations are adopted that combine the best characteristics of those existing. What appears to be an either-or decision requires thinking out of the box.

- If my son loved me, he would do as I ask and join the priesthood. But he did not do as I asked. Therefore, he doesn't love me!

A thinly-veiled manipulative tactic by some of the people we most care about sometimes equates a personal choice with a show of familial love. The choice of vocation or calling cannot signify proof of love or loyalty. The very choice on this basis negates the nature of the choice as a vocation. Personal choice and family love cannot be juxtaposed against each other. A son can still love his parents whatever vocation he chooses.

In each of these examples, there is always another alternative, although there is an implicit false premise that only the two choices exist – the black and the white – and that they are mutually exclusive.

Addressing The Fallacy

The fallacy can be easily detected by the either-or premise laid. When faced with this argument, examine closely whether the choices truly exclude each other and if there are no other alternatives available. This will open one's eyes to many other possible decisions.

The Black-and-White fallacy involves two extremes and the gray area in between. It is often confused with the next fallacy, and we will explain how they differ.

8. Middle Ground

When someone argues that the so-called "middle ground" between two extremes is correct simply because it is somewhere between the extremes. The claim about the middle ground is best is not based on the superior merit of that middle alternative over the extremes. Rather, it is a compromise between them with possibly less merit. It is offered as the best choice under the presumption that advocates of the extreme alternatives may find it acceptable for all.

- Vincent likes Annie, who dances ballet in the theatre. But Vincent's mom wants to match him with Delia, the owner of a local restaurant. To settle the matter, Vincent's dad introduced him to Angela, a dancer at a bar-and-grill.

Vincent's dad erroneously presumes that Vincent likes Anna because she dances, and his mom prefers Delia because she works in the restaurant business. He is oblivious to the type of dance or the nature of the restaurant job. He does not think that the best choice may actually be Annie, who Vincent may like for her many other qualities.

- Andrew is a Republican who felt he could not tolerate a Democrat governor. His wife, Priscila, is a Democrat who felt she could not tolerate a Republican governor. To keep the peace, they decided to vote for the Independent candidate.

The best choice for governor should be the candidate most qualified to discharge the office's duties; this should be the premise when deciding the elected official. Therefore, choosing based on the party does not guarantee the best choice. It is possible that one of the other major party candidates would have made a better choice.

- Bruno used to drink ten bottles of beer a day. After ten years of this, he got sick and required angioplasty to open up an artery. The doctor gave him strict orders not to drink a single drop ever again because it was bad for his health. When Bruno got home, he thought to himself, "I'm afraid to die, but I can't go without beer!" So, he decided to drink just five bottles a day.

In many medical cases, doctors will allow patients some leeway in alcohol consumption, but they will recommend complete abstinence in serious cases. Strict orders from a doctor allow for no compromise for the good of the patient. Bruno did not understand that the middle position in this case – from the doctor's advice not to drink a single drop to his former ten bottle consumption daily – or five bottles a day, is an unacceptable decision.

The Middle Ground fallacy and Black-and-White fallacy are similar as far as they both involve either choosing one of the extremes or a compromise between them. The difference is that in the black-and-white fallacy, the middle choice may be the best, while in the Middle Ground fallacy, one of the extremes is likely the better choice

Addressing The Fallacy

The middle ground fallacy is also easy to spot because the proposition involves a compromise between two alternative extreme positions. The compromise is patently inadequate or inappropriate to address the issue raised. The decision was made for no other reason than that the choice was the middle ground. To address this fallacy, analyze the choices on their merits, and any compromise made should consider the merits.

9. False Cause

The false cause fallacy exists in arguments where the logical connection between the premises and the conclusion is an imaginary link. There are three types of false-cause fallacies based on three types of erroneous logical connections.

9.1 Post Hoc Ergo Propter Hoc ("After This, Therefore Because Of This")

- After every thunderstorm, the grass in the golf course looks greener, therefore, thunderstorms cause the grass to be greener.

It is not actually the thunderstorms per se that make the grass greener, but the grass was watered. Turning on the sprinkler systems will typically have the same outcome.

- She throws up after every public speech she makes; therefore making speeches cause her to throw up.

It is not the speech that makes her throw up, but the stress she feels that makes her feel nauseous after every public presentation. She may benefit from some professional advice or public speaking classes to0, or undertake some mental exercises to destress before her speech, but she should not avoid her speaking engagements.

- After the Aztecs performed rituals offering human sacrifices to the gods, their harvests were bountiful. Therefore, the sacrifices brought the bountiful harvests.

The concurrence between sacrificial offerings and the bountiful harvests is circumstantial since agricultural science has already laid the requisites for a more bountiful harvest. Human sacrifice does not influence harvest productivity, and it is an unnecessary and horrendous waste of human life.

- My office rival Sandra gave the boss a nice Christmas gift, and in January, she was promoted. Wow, that gift sure paid a lot of dividends!

The gift Sandra gave and her subsequent promotion may or may not have a causal relation, but no conclusion is possible absent substantial proof. Sandra may have been in line for a promotion for years based on her good work. To judge that she was promoted just because of the gift is mean-spirited and in poor taste.

9.2 Cum Hoc Ergo Propter Hoc ("With This, Therefore Because Of This")

- When dogs go for a walk, they poop on the sidewalk; therefore, it is the walk that causes them to poop.

Going for a walk may provide dogs the exercise they need to relieve themselves, but dogs are known to relieve themselves even when they are confined to closed spaces.

Some dogs don't relieve themselves at all during walks. It is not the walk that causes the evacuation but the dog's own bodily functions.

- When John plays music while fishing, he catches fish, playing the music attracts fish so John could catch them.

Music may or may not influence the fish, but to conclude, this would require scientific research possible with the help of an experiment. There are too many factors present in the outdoors that influence fishing. What can be determined for certain is whether John enjoys the music while he goes fishing because John can respond concerning how he feels about the music. Otherwise, there is no logical link between the music and the number of fish caught.

- While traveling in their RV, a couple's dog kept howling in his traveling case. They thought that the dog was disturbed by the trip and did not enjoy riding along. It took the dog whisperer to convince the couple that the wife Ana's anxiety was causing the dog's distress.

People often mistakenly interpret their dog's actions depending on how she reacts to ongoing stimuli. However, dog behaviorists and psychologists explain that dogs act the way they do in response to their owner's emotions. The relationship between a dog and its master is not common knowledge, so an expert may sometimes need to explain the truth to dispel laymen's misconceptions.

9.3 Ignoring Common Cause

This fallacy refers to the belief that one thing caused something while ignoring the possibility that another thing may have caused both things.

- I thought that the roosters' crowing in the morning wakes the rest of the farm animals up. But the last rooster died, and all the animals woke up anyway. So, the rising sun wakes all the animals up on the farm, including the roosters.

It is a charming element in stories about farm life that attributes the waking of the animals to the cock's crow. The truth is that diurnal animals will wake with the sunrise, whether the rooster crows or not.

- Rising inflation caused interest rates to rise. Actually, economic policies tend to cause both inflation and interest rates to fluctuate.

Economic analysts expect interest rates to rise when inflation rates go up. This is true because the monetary authority uses its policies to control the money supply. But there have been times when increasing inflation does not result in increasing interest rates. Economic indicators respond to the effects of broad economic policies.

- The homicide rate is increasing, which the mayor blames on the rise in illegal firearms in the city. She should admit that they are both the result of poor law enforcement under her watch.

This fallacy is independent of people's views on gun control. The clue lies in the words of the argument itself. Both homicide and the possession of illegal firearms are against the law. The number of illegal firearms is not the ultimate cause of the rise in homicides, which could be carried out by means other than a gun. But both point to lax law enforcement, which is the true cause of the rising crime rate.

Addressing The Fallacy

The false cause fallacy can be difficult to identify because for some cases, the subject may be nuanced and require special knowledge (e.g., dog psychology and economics in the previous examples). Sometimes, they are easy to detect because they openly defy logic (e.g., human sacrifice). To address false cause fallacies involving difficult issues or claims, you must do some research and consult reliable experts about the true causes of some phenomena. Combine both logic and information to resolve a false cause fallacy.

. . .

10. Red Herring

This fallacy occurs when the arguer throws out an irrelevant issue to distract and confuse the listener into agreeing with the claim. The name comes from a practice escaping prisoners allegedly did during prison breaks. They threw the odorous red herrings in different directions to distract the chasing dogs away from their human scent and off their trail. In this fallacy, the red herring is the irrelevant issue [22].

- Ian was caught driving the wrong way down a one-way street. Oblivious of the nearby street signs, Ian's response to the arresting officer was, "But officer, I did not know this was a one-way street." The officer asked for his driver's license, which turned out to be expired. "Really? I was not aware!" Finally, the officer told Ian that the car he was driving was reported stolen. "No, you don't say! I borrowed this car from my friend, but I just forgot to ask his permission."

All three reasons Ian gave were red herrings. First, ignorance of the law excuses no one. Second, all drivers should be responsible for their documents. Third, possessing another person's property without permission creates a presumption of theft. So, all three reasons given by Ian are irrelevant to his defense.

Here are other common red herring fallacies.

- Teacher, the dog ate my homework.

The dog eating one's homework is irrelevant. Prudence dictates one should always have a copy for submission. No homework still means no grade.

  - I'm sure there is no global warming, The ice age we learned about in the seventies hasn't even come yet.

One scientific theory's validity cannot hinge on the validity of another, possibly irrelevant, scientific theory. Citing one debunked theory to disprove another theory is a red herring.

  - Hollywood types are not trustworthy. Actors and actresses know how to pretend, so they can make you believe anything.

The artistic portrayal of other people is not tantamount to deception and therefore is irrelevant to weighing the trustworthiness of people.

  - When the majority of Marvel superheroes were killed off in Avengers: Infinity War [23], there was a spike in grief counseling sessions by fans upset with the demise of their favorite stars. Therefore, films with tragic endings are unhealthy for the viewing public and should be outlawed by media regulators.

Confusion of on-screen personas and the actors who play them happen more frequently now that visual entertainment has approached new heights in realism. But avid fans possibly take "suspension of belief" to extremes. Using transient abnormal reactions to justify censorship of the media is a red herring.

Addressing The Fallacy

Since a red herring aims to distract and confuse, resist being distracted and confused. You should suspect a red herring when you feel that the argument makes no sense. Since the issue the arguer raises makes no sense, ignore it altogether and go straight to a resolution. (The officer in the first example should simply give Ian a ticket.) You do not need to argue down a foolish proposition.

11. Slippery Slope

The slippery slope fallacy argues that taking one small step, although seemingly harmless, would eventually lead one to increasingly harmful situations. This is why the first step should not be taken at all. The "slippery slope" is that unavoidable path towards more danger, even when there may be no strong reason for this to happen [24].

- Marijuana is a gateway drug. Once you get used to it, you'll look for methamphetamine, cocaine, then heroin, in search of new highs.

Cannabis is not justified as a gateway drug. The research established that the vast majority of those who used marijuana does not necessarily progress to more potent substance abuse [25].

- Don't even think that it's okay to tell white lies. You'll get used to telling bigger and bigger lies until you can't tell the truth anymore.

Some research tends to support this, but research also suggests social lying (white lies), which is sometimes resorted to because people fear inflicting emotional harm with an honest but negative comment [26]. Compassion is the driver for some white lies, suggesting that people cease to lie in other situations where the altruistic motivation is absent.

- We should guard our liberties against encroachment by an increasingly tyrannical government. Today, it's masks and lockdowns. Tomorrow they'll come after our freedom of speech and religion. We should not give an inch.

This rather dramatic suggestion of masks gradually encroaching upon the eventual abolition of the bill of rights is somewhat far fetched but not entirely irrelevant. It is a slippery-slope fallacy because of its allegation that wearing a mask (i.e., to avoid disease contamination) will eventually lead to dictatorship, a speculation without reliable proof,

Addressing The Fallacy

A slippery slope fallacy may be countered by proving that the alleged future outcome is not the necessary conclusion. Research, such as the survey conducted for the use of cannabis or narration of past events that ended up with different results, may rebut the fallacious argument.

12. False Analogy

This type of fallacy draws a false comparison between two things. It states that if A and B are the same regarding a certain quality, they must also be the same regarding other qualities. The next three arguments are false analogy fallacies because the criterion for comparison does not support the conclusion.

- Timmy and Tommy are both Navy Seals.
  Tommy is a good husband and father. That
  means Timmy will likewise be a good husband
  and father.

Timmy and Tommy being Navy Seals may mean they are both well-trained, but this has no bearing on their inclinations for marriage and family.

- Filipinos and Indonesians are both warm,

hospitable Asians. Filipinos are mostly Catholic. Indonesians are, therefore, mostly Catholic, too.

Filipinos and Indonesians are closely related ethnically and culturally, but their historical difference resulted in Indonesia being mostly Muslim and the Philippines being predominantly Catholic.

- Aspirin is a French invention. So was the guillotine. Aspirin is beneficial to mankind; therefore, the guillotine must also be just as beneficial to mankind.

Inventions made in the same country may be good or bad depending on their use. Aspirin is a medicine to alleviate pain, while the guillotine is an instrument for mass executions.

The false analogy can refer to two items or persons in the same category but with different levels of the same characteristic. The analogy fails because a different reason underlies the same thing being compared.

- Dr. Phillip caught his student Jill opening her handbook during a test. He called her attention and asked her why she was cheating. "I'm not cheating, Doctor. When I was your intern, I noticed that you consulted your handbook when you wrote a prescription for a patient. Since you're already a doctor but still have to read your handbook, then I think I should be able to do the same since I am still a student and much less knowledgeable than you."

Dr. Phillip consulting his handbook is an act of diligence to ensure that he is providing the right treatment for his patient. That is part of due diligence. Jill, on the other hand, is a student who is taking an exam to test her knowledge. Therefore, Dr. Phillip is right to prohibit her from consulting her handbook because it will defeat the purpose of the test. Their purposes for doing the same are not comparable.

- My wife forbids me from drinking because she says alcohol is the drink of the devil. I don't see what's wrong with it. Our parish priest is a saint compared to me, and he drinks wine in front of the whole congregation every Sunday.

The husband drinks wine as an act of self-indulgence. The priest drinks the wine during mass as part of the celebration of a religious sacrament. The act of drinking wine in the two cases is not comparable.

Addressing The Fallacy

Again, it might not be easy to spot a false analogy fallacy because you will need to analyze the thing being compared. If the criteria for comparison are not relevant to the conclusion, then it is a false analogy and disregarded.

13. Sunk Cost Fallacy

The term "sunk cost" in economic terms refers to an investment that has already been made. The sunk cost fallacy pertains to a person's behavior due to investing time, effort, or money on something [27]. The conclusion they arrive at is for them to "get their money's worth," to try to derive the value of what they had invested even if it may put them at a further disadvantage.

Another name for this fallacy is the Concorde Fallacy. It is an open reference to the Concorde supersonic airliner whose project proponents continued to pursue even though the future returns were bound to be unstable [28]. Sunk cost relates to loss aversion (the psychological pain of incurring a loss) and status quo bias (the urge to keep things as they are) [29].

- Chris already spent a lot of money dating Shiela in terms of fancy lobster dinners, Broadway plays, and expensive gifts. He now expects her to accept his marriage proposal because he deserves it, after all the money and time he gave her.

The fallacy in this argument rests in the implication that Shiela owes it to Chris to accept his proposal because he already spent a large sum in courting her. However, the true justification for accepting the proposal should be her willingness to become his spouse. A variation of this case is more sinister:

- Ron is going out on a hot new date. He's going to treat her to a movie, a lobster dinner, and expensive drinks. He's hoping that he'll get his money's worth if she invites him up afterward.

Courting expenses should not be relevant to the acceptance of a more permanent relationship. Even more so, the price of a date should not be the reason to expect an after-date romance.

- Randy bought a membership in a resort hotel where he agrees to pay a fixed amount to use the property for two weeks a year. At first, he thought this was a good idea. Later on, Randy felt that he did not want to vacation in the same place every year, or even vacation. But since he already paid for it, Randy continued staying in that resort home for two weeks every year.

Randy has several options, such as exchanging this membership with others selling off his share at a slight discount if he wanted to. But Randy wanted to get the value of his money and so went on vacations he did not really want.

- Despite having tried the catering business for a year, it was obvious that this was a failing venture from the start. Still, Alice insisted on pushing on, reasoning she still wanted to recover what she already invested.

This last situation is much the same as the Concorde project, where the project proponents refuse to give up on the dream. Alice refuses to admit that the business was a bad idea and still looks to recover though it is highly unlikely.

Sunk cost fallacies are relatively easy to identify because they involve investing some discernible value in terms of time, money or effort, and refusing to take a loss on it when that would have been a more sensible decision. However, the sunk cost dilemma is not as easy to resolve because it is essentially behavioral.

Addressing The Fallacy

The best decision-making guide to avoid getting caught up in a sunk cost fallacy trap is to set a cut-loss limit when investing, and having the discipline to follow this plan if it materializes. A cut-loss limit is a point at which one is willing to assume a loss – 20% of the investment value, one year into the venture, or any measure in time and resources. Having set this, one should develop the resolve to cut clean when that point is reached, and not look back in regret.

.   .   .

14. Appeal To The People

This type of fallacy relies on the listeners' desire to be associated with a large group of people or people of a particular type as the basis for persuasion. There are three such fallacies: the Bandwagon Fallacy, Appeal to Vanity, and Appeal to Snobbery, but the Bandwagon Fallacy is the more popular of the three [30].

14.1 Bandwagon Fallacy

As the name suggests, this fallacy seeks to persuade the listener to accept a claim because many others accept it.

- The year's best-selling car in the United States is the Ford F-Series, so you should consider buying one.

Purchasing a vehicle is expensive. Therefore, the buyer should be guided by the reason for the purchase when choosing what to buy. Just citing it as the best-selling car does not say anything about cost-effectiveness, performance, or special features (i.e., four-wheel drive) that the owner might particularly like.

- Everybody uses credit cards for online transactions these days, so it must be pretty safe.

Not everybody uses credit cards, and in certain applications, it is not safe, as the rising instances of card shows. The popularity of a particular service or product does not prove it is safe, therefore, precautions must be ensured.

14.2 Appeal To Vanity

When the argument associates the claim with a preferred status or lifestyle, it is an Appeal to Vanity.

- Men who lift weights and build their muscles attract more women at the beach. If you want to be a ladies' man, do gym workouts three times a week.

A specified frequency of gym workouts does not guarantee that a man will attract more women. Many women are attracted to men who are smart, charming, and amiable. A well-defined physique may be an image that a gym enthusiast may work towards as its own reward.

- If you eat only plant-based food and avoid meat, you will not only become healthier but happier. There are benefits to becoming a vegetarian.

Slim and healthy is an image one can work towards, but it is the person's disposition that will eventually determine whether or not he/she will be happy.

· · ·

14.3 Appeal to Snobbery

Another common argument links the claim to being a part of an elite group. This is known as Appeal to Snobbery.

- A graduate from Harvard is respected as an intellectual giant, therefore, I will go there for my college degree.

The choice of school should depend on the enrollee's selected degree and his/her parent's ability to pay. Going to an expensive school for bragging rights is impractical and unwise.

- You should accept his marriage proposal. He is the prince, so you will be a princess and live happily ever after.

Agreeing to marry to gain a title does not bring happiness. This has been born out of several real-life personalities. The conclusion does not logically follow the premise.

Appeal to Vanity and Appeal to Snobbery are quite similar, but they differ in intention. The Appeal to Snobbery aims to convince the listener to acquire a desirable status by joining an elite group. In contrast, the Appeal to Vanity aims more to convince the listener to adopt a desirable lifestyle.

· · ·

Addressing The Fallacy

The appeal to people or popularity fallacy is misleading because it substitutes a reference group's opinion for our own. It implies that we cannot decide for ourselves, so we accept others'"better sense" to decide for us. When faced with this argument, we must decide what degree we wish to be defined by that reference group. The best choice is, always, to decide according to our best lights.

15. Straw Man

This fallacy gives the illusion of refuting the proposition being made when the argument covertly replaces the original proposition with another, weaker proposition ("the straw man") and attacks that instead. This leaves the original proposition cunningly unaddressed.

15.1 Distortion

Distortion substitutes the real issue with an entirely different and unfounded issue that totally misrepresents the situation.

- Your daughter Daisy complimented my son Robert on his family's history and status. She obviously wants to marry my son because he comes from a rich and socially respected family. She is merely interested in our wealth and fame.

Therefore, this wedding should not push through.

Many parents in families of high social stature have made this straw man's argument. The arguer confounds the genuine respect and appreciation shown by Daisy with the accusation of having a shallow interest in their social standing and affluence. By ascribing this malicious intention to Daisy, Robert's parents can make their objection to the wedding more acceptable.

- Arlyne wanted to join the volleyball team, but her mom informed the coach that she does not have her parents' permission. "Her arm was fractured when she was younger, and her doctor advised against her playing competitively until her bones are stronger." When her coach told Arlyne, she vented her anger against her mother. "You're always against everything I want. You just don't want me to be happy!"

Parents, as a rule, want their children to pursue their dreams, but occasionally there is a good reason for them to call a halt. Older children may feel resentful when their elders tell them, "No," and lash out by distorting the issue and painting their parents as domineering. This makes them feel justified in their rebellion.

15.2 Oversimplification

For this straw man, the larger issue becomes minimized to cover only a portion of it or only one of many contributory factors,

- McDonald's serves very hot coffee. My client positioned the coffee cup between her knees as she took the lid off her coffee cup. The scalding hot coffee spilled on her, and she had third-degree burns requiring a visit to the emergency room. The warning sign printed on the side of the cup is so tiny that anyone can hardly see it, but it proves McDonald's knows its coffee is very hot. The accident is, therefore, McDonald's fault.

In this instance, many contributing factors led to the customer's injury. The lawyer arguing the case disregards his client's lack of care and her failure to take precautions, instead of simplifying the issue to McDonald's making the coffee too hot. It is more complicated because the customer's negligence contributed to the accident.

- To determine custody of the children in a divorce proceeding, the parent who is better off financially and has a steady source of income should be given sole custody of the children. It is for the children's benefit.

The complex considerations involved in parental custody include the children's welfare, the parties' parental skills, their availability to tend to the children, the proximity of the residence to school and hospital, community conditions for raising children, etc. Making it a matter of who has more money is an oversimplification of a complicated decision.

15.3 Overextension

Whereas oversimplification reduces the scope of the issues involved, overextension includes issues related but not relevant to the true issue involved to direct the cause elsewhere.

- When the suspect was a boy, he was abandoned
  by his parents. He became a ward of the state
  and transferred from one foster home to another.
  He did not receive the proper upbringing and
  moral instruction that all children are entitled to.
  Now that he has committed a crime, it is not his
  fault but the fault of the state.

The failures of the foster care system do not negate the personal responsibility of all mature individuals over their own actions. Others have gone through the same system and emerged as responsible adults, even taking the initiative to reform the system based on their experiences [31]. The suspect in the above case remains culpable.

- Modern high-rise buildings are energy inefficient
  and, therefore, contribute significantly to the
  city's carbon footprint, a major cause of climate

change. Therefore, the city council should order a retrofitting of all its high-rise buildings. Its energy sources should use only solar and wind.

In a case of overreach, new regulations should not work retroactively to include changes to structure compliant with the code existing at the time. It becomes a penalty to property owners who will need to undertake expensive repairs for no fault on their part.

Addressing The Fallacy

To identify a straw man fallacy, remember a fine line between a reasonably reformulated argumentative criticism and a strategically concocted straw man [32]. The arguer misrepresents the opponent's strong proposition and substitutes it with a weak one. The arguer successfully attacks the weaker proposition while ignoring the original claim. Distortion, oversimplification, or extension beyond the claim's original limits results in duplicity [33].

16. Appeal To Force

The Appeal to Force is similar to Appeal to Fear, except that in the former, the arguer threatens the harm, while in the latter the fear is inspired by a source other than the arguer.

Strictly speaking, an Appeal to Force is not a fallacious argument or an argument at all [34] because it does not rely on logic but coercion. However, it rightly earned its place among the fallacies because it effectively wins arguments when the side threatening force is losing the logical debate.

- Wally told Ida that if she insists on working as an airline attendant, he will call the wedding off.

From an independent perspective, this is an appeal for force. Deciding to marry should be based on whether two people feel so strongly about each other to want to live their lives together "for better or for worse, for richer or poorer, in sickness and in health," so what their occupations are should not matter to each other.

The threat is, therefore, for Wally to force Ida to do what he wants. However, if Wally were to issue such a groundless threat, then this gives Ida a reason to call off the wedding herself. Obviously, Wally is not into it "for better or worse."

- You better believe that climate change exists, or we will put you on social media as a denier [35].

This particular appeal to force applies to nearly all unpopular acts any person with a social media presence may commit. Online bullying has become an effective threat that can "persuade" anybody to comply even if the appeal goes unsaid.

- In the sixties, we strictly complied with our

father's orders, or else he threatened to spank us with his leather belt.

The threat of corporal punishment is an Appeal to Force as children could not question parental authority. Logic does not play a role in this type of strict upbringing.

The threat of force mustn't be the one that is reasonable or normal to expect in light of the premise. If the "threat" is actually a fact or reasonable consequence of the conclusion, then the argument becomes logical. The following are examples of such non-fallacies.

- I am an IRS agent. Make sure to report all your income, or I will have to come after you.
- You have to submit your thesis before starting the Christmas break, or I will give you a failing grade.
- If you don't brush your teeth every day, tooth decay will set in. I'll have to take you to the dentist, who will have to pull out all your rotting teeth!

Addressing The Fallacy

This fallacy can be identified by the nature of the act the arguer threatens to inflict upon the listener. The consequence of non-compliance or failure to agree has no logical link to the argument. The only way to counter the fallacy is to use logical reasoning to explain why the agreement is impossible. Remember, though, that standing your ground may result in the infliction of the harm threatened. If the risk is great and the harm is severe, recourse to a legal remedy might be necessary.

17. Fallacy Fallacy

Also known as the Argument from Fallacy, this fallacy relies on the justification that since the claim was argued poorly (i.e., the argument rests on a fallacy), that the claim itself is wrong when in fact, it may be right.

- Cecilia told Susan that turmeric tea cured her arthritic knees, but Susan later found out that Cecilia had knee surgery. Susan now believes that turmeric tea really has no benefit for arthritis.

The fallacious assertion is that Cecilia's knees healed completely due to turmeric. This is an overstatement, as turmeric reasonably claims only to alleviate, not cure, the condition. Susan commits another fallacy in completely denying any benefits turmeric may have.

- Alan wanted a dog. His parents heard that dogs make good pets because some dogs, like Yorkshire terriers, don't cause asthma. They got Alan a French bulldog, which unfortunately worsened his asthma. The parents decided that dogs do not make good pets after all.

The claim is that dogs make good pets, which is true since dogs are man's best friend. The initial fallacy is that dogs make good pets because they don't cause asthma. This is a hasty generalization fallacy because only some dogs are hypoallergenic.

The fallacy fallacy is that simply because it is not true that all dogs don't cause asthma, then all dogs don't make good pets. Sadly, this unsound reasoning may deny Alan the love of a dog he may have dearly wanted.

Addressing The Fallacy

Fallacy fallacy is a type of fallacy that logic enthusiasts are prone to fall for. Those who are aware of fallacies may tend to focus on identifying fallacies and, finding some, may dismiss the conclusion as false even if it may be true,

To counter the fallacy fallacy, identify why the original argument is fallacious and address the flaw in its logic. If this original fallacy came from you, then acknowledge that it is logically flawed. Then you should show that the fallacious reasoning does not negate or invalidate the principal claim in the original argument. The next step would be to retract the fallacious claim in the original argument, leaving the valid conclusion intact.

Bringing It All Together

The number and variety of fallacies we have encountered in this short discussion demonstrate how common fallacies are and how frequently we encounter them. These are but a few of the hundreds of possible logical errors identified by the scholars of logic.

It is impossible to remember them all, and even if we do, we may not be able to identify them as quickly as we encounter them. Being aware of only a fraction of them and practicing as much as possible in spotting them daily will nevertheless hone our skills in thinking, discussing, and deciding.

Action Steps

Informal fallacies are everywhere in popular literature. Choose an article or two from a favorite magazine, online website, or the opinion or society page of a newspaper. Scan the article while applying the following steps, devised by Vaidya and Erickson [36], and see how many fallacies you can find.

1. Examine if the passage contains an argument; if so, state the conclusion. Knowing the conclusion is the first step to analyzing its logical supports.

2. Determine if the passage contains a controversial claim. The current debate about them usually suggests the issues around controversies.

3. Examine whether any of the central claims rely on expertise. Gather the established expert knowledge and opinions as well as matters that are still unsettled.

4. Explore whether options or alternatives suggested by the passage are exhaustive.

5. Consider carefully whether any of the words may signify different things. Watch out for double meanings and words used in different contexts.

Remember, some passages contain more than one fallacy, so patience and persistence will go a long way.

How Well Can You Spot The Fallacy?

In the following exercise, five situations describe arguments that may or may not be fallacious. Analyze whether a fallacy is involved, and if so, which type of fallacy. Explain your answer. The solution appears at the end of this chapter.

A. They said a flu epidemic is currently spreading over the country. However, in our town, there is no sign of the flu. Therefore, it is not true that there is such an epidemic.

B. The family is the building block of a well-founded society because a healthy society's foundation rests on communities composed of strong families.

C. Every time I visit my Chinese friend's store, his business quickly picks up after, so he calls me his lucky charm and invites me to visit often.

D. The same company that handles the Disney theme parks' advertising campaign also does the advertising for the carnival rides in our town. I am sure that our rides are just as safe as those in the Disney parks.

E. John called in sick, so his boss Alan gave him the day off. At noon, Alan went to the nearby mall for lunch. There he saw John with his wife. Alan asked a little pointedly, "John, I thought you were sick." John replied, "My doctor's clinic is on the fourth floor."

Moving On

Informal fallacies result from unsound reasoning just as formal fallacies result from construction errors in framing arguments. Many logical mistakes are impulsive - like parents' mental panic attacks when their pre-schooler mentions "sex." But some are wickedly intended to mislead and confuse. Therefore, it is important to know how to avoid such errors, which the final chapter will discuss.

Key Takeaways

- Informal fallacies are created by unsound reasoning.

- Some fallacies rely on weak evidence, such as appeals to emotion, authority, and the people.
- Others are fallacies of weak induction, such as straw men, red herrings, middle ground, and false causes.
- Still, others are fallacies of ambiguity that make a weak connection between premises and conclusion, such as begging the question, slippery slopes, false analogy, and appeal to force.

Solution To The Exercise:

1. Appeal to Ignorance
2. Begging the Question
3. False Cause, Post Hoc Ergo Propter Hoc
4. False Analogy
5. No Fallacy

6

MAKING THE CHANGE: HOW CAN WE BECOME RATIONAL THINKERS?

> *The most difficult subjects can be explained to the most slow-witted man if he has not formed any idea of them already; but the simplest thing cannot be made clear to the most intelligent man if he is firmly persuaded that he knows already, without a shadow of a doubt, what is laid before him.*[1]

— LEO TOLSTOY, THE KINGDOM OF GOD IS WITHIN YOU, P. 49

In the poem by John Godrey Sage, "The Blind Men and the Elephant" [2], there were six men of Indostan who went to "see" their first elephant. The fact that all of them were blind led to some interesting outcomes when they encountered this magnificent beast. For those who are unfamiliar with the story, here's a quick summary.

The six men approached the elephant from six directions and therefore touched different parts of its body. The first touched its broadside and said that the elephant was like a wall. The second felt its tusk and pronounced that it was like a spear. The third held its trunk and said it was like a snake, and the fourth felt its knee and said it was like a tree. The fifth touched the ear and announced that it was like a fan, and the sixth groped its swinging tail and exclaimed that the elephant was like a rope.

To the six blind men of Indostan, the elephant was six different things. And it is a good bet that none of them could convince the others that the elephant was anything other than what they came to conclude for themselves.

Now, none of them were lying. They were very sincere because they based their opinions on their first-hand experience. All of them perceived the truth, but only a portion of it. None of them appreciated the whole truth, not having had the opportunity to examine the whole elephant.

Leo Tolstoy was convinced that people whose minds resembled a blank slate could be taught anything, but those who have their own experiences would have difficulty accepting a different view from others. In short, we are biased in favor of what we already know to be true. Overcoming that bias requires evidence and logical persuasion, yet some prefer to cling to their biases even with the best arguments.

But before we discuss biases, let's recall the logical concepts in the previous chapters.

Recalling The Key Concepts

Humans are rational beings. We use our reasoning to make sense of our surroundings, and what we learn through reason we commit to memory. Reasoning is instinctive and informal. Logic is systematic reasoning according to the principles of validity. All people reason, but not all people do it logically. Logic enables us to structure our reasoning into arguments, composed of premises and a conclusion. Arguments are the means to convey ideas logically. Their main goal is to persuade others of the truth of one's claim.

Not all arguments are valid, and even if they were not all valid arguments are sound. Some arguments do not lead to the truth; they are fallacious. Fallacies are defects in arguments that result from unsound reasoning. Some fallacies are logical mistakes and are therefore unintentional. However, some fallacies are devices unscrupulously employed by insincere arguers to win the discussion but not seek the truth.

In the real world, our decision-making processes involve dealing with arguments within ourselves and with other persons. We weigh the claims and their proofs to resolve multiple levels of complex arguments. The process is difficult and often confusing. We are often tempted to fall back on past experiences and stock knowledge to make short-cuts in arriving at a decision. It is in making such short-cuts that our biases take over, leading us to often make the wrong decision.

Recognizing Our Biases

Thinking rationally involves consistently abiding by logical principles, whether we do so intentionally or instinctively. Sometimes, we fail to apply these principles due to biases that we are subject to. A few of them are discussed here.

1. Confirmation Bias

This is one of the most common biases that we are all probably guilty of. We tend to favor ideas that confirm our existing opinions and the information we already accept as truth. It refers to "unwitting selectivity in the acquisition and use of evidence," an "unwitting molding of facts to fit" one's beliefs [3]. Philosophers and psychologists have determined that people find it easier to accept claims that align more closely with what they already believe to be true, rather than those propositions they want to be false.

Confirmation bias in real-world contexts exists in the fields of policy rationalization (politics), medicine, judicial reasoning, and science, among others. For instance, traditional Chinese would prefer to be cured through acupuncture and the application of Chinese herbs and medicines rather than Western forms of treatment. Confirmation bias exists because people want to believe, because their frames of reference are already conditioned, and people have a pragmatic desire to avoid error [4].

2. First Impression Bias

This type of bias refers to "a limitation of human information processing in which people are strongly influenced by the first piece of information that they are exposed to, and they are biased in evaluating subsequent information in the direction of the initial influence" [5]. Studies have shown that first impressions are formed around certain constructs in social cognition, such as character traits, trustworthiness, and competence; facial appearance, and simple behaviors (e.g. judging one is possibly lazy or slow-witted), or their goals, values, and beliefs.

In the real world, first impression bias is often manifested during the personnel recruitment or hiring process. Employers tend to ask questions that confirm their first impressions about the candidates and treat them accordingly [6]. The way to avoid first impression bias is to suspend judgment after the first few meetings and wait until all relative information is available before concluding.

. . .

3. The Dunning-Kruger Effect

In 1999, Kruger and Dunning [7] observed that in many social and intellectual domains, people generally have an overly favorable opinion of their abilities. They suggest that this overestimation takes place partly because those who are unskilled in such domains tend to carry a dual burden. First, they reach faulty conclusions and make erroneous choices. Second, they are unaware that they are doing so because their incompetence hinders their metacognitive ability to realize it. "Metacognition" is knowledge of one's thinking and learning, an awareness of their own higher-order thinking skills [8].

Most people are deficient in their metacognition that they exhibit a bias towards the validity of their own erroneous beliefs. An example would be students' assessment of how they performed in an exam or class activity. When they receive a failing grade, they are convinced it is unfair and argue that they deserve a higher grade. To avoid the Dunning-Kruger bias, the metacognitive competence of individuals may be improved by improving their skills and recognizing their limitations in the specific domain.

4. Fundamental Attribution Error (Fae)

This type of bias is a social error involving an overestimation of an actor's personality while at the same time underestimating the situational factors when trying to explain the cause of an event or behavior [9]. According to the study by Berry, we tend to commit the FAE many times a day. A typical example is when an employee comes late to work and is reprimanded by her manager. That same manager arrives late at a subsequent meeting and offers excuses for being late. More recently are the frequent occurrences of officials chastising and sanctioning people in their jurisdictions who failed to comply with local orders and who themselves are found violating the same orders they were enforcing on their constituents.

The FAE is typically an error caused by somebody using limited information to make judgments. There are several things one may do to avoid the FAE. One is to list down five good qualities of the individual towards whom you are beginning to feel resentful. Practice empathy by discussing with other people about their lives and getting to know them better. Broaden your perspective and examine the situation more closely before passing judgment about the actors in it. Develop self-awareness and objectivity in assessing behavior and happenings [10].

5. Decline Bias (Declinism)

This bias tends to view the past as overly positive and the present or future in an extremely negative light. This bias is typically applied to one's view of a country, society, institution, or any similarly general context. Humans have a propensity to focus more on negative information than positive information, such as conveyed in the news, and this negativity shapes the worldview of some people [11]. Declinism is a negativity bias, a feeling shared by many that their society is in decline [12].

Part of declinism is the tendency to romanticize the past. Men and women who grew up in the 50s and 60s may feel that men and women's traditional roles (men worked, women kept the home and raised the children) reflected a much better time because lives were simpler. Today the opposite is likely to happen, that women who chose to stay at home full time are scorned because their gender is now expected to balance career and family.

The first step towards avoiding declinism is to be aware of our emotional attachments to the past. From that awareness, a greater focus should be devoted to the positive things in the present surroundings [13]. Go so far as to make a list of how society is better now than in the past. When some things are worse off today, keep a reminder that the difficulties today are merely challenges, not a sign that an apocalypse is approaching.

6. Diagnostic Bias

Also known as diagnostic suspicion bias or provider bias, diagnostic bias occurs when one's perception, prejudice, or subjective judgment affects one's diagnosis. As its name suggests, this is a bias committed by medical or health professionals. These are the professionals who diagnose illnesses or injuries by examining the symptoms or diagnostic tests results. Knowledge of exposure to some chemical agent or contagious disease are examples of factors that may influence the perception of a physician in making her diagnosis. She may schedule tests or look for specific symptoms in that group that she would not normally do for a non-exposed group [14].

The diagnostic bias is a specialized category that traces its causes back to the more generic types of bias, including anchoring, availability, confirmation, framing, and premature closure biases. The following are the descriptions and corrective strategies for the types of bias that form the root causes of diagnostic bias [15].

• *Anchoring* – Sticking with a diagnosis after it is debunked. The health professional will insist on continuing treatment consistent with the first diagnosis instead of adopting a treatment more appropriate to the real malady. The corrective strategy is to examine the patient's unresponsiveness or seek new information to refine the original diagnosis.

• *Availability* – The professional refers to what most readily comes to mind. The physician makes a diagnosis similar to that of a previous patient who manifests the same symptoms. A more alert professional would know the statistical likelihood and baseline prevalence of the diagnosed condition.

• *Confirmation* – Applied specifically to diagnostic bias, confirmation bias refers to the preference for findings that support an already-suspected diagnosis or strategy. For instance, urine test results that may indicate another condition are taken to confirm the patient's self-diagnosis of a kidney infection. The countervailing strategy is to refer to an objective source such as a diagnostic checklist) in evaluating how strongly the diagnosis matches the technical findings.

• *Framing* – Refers to gathering or assembling elements that support a particular diagnosis. An example is assuming that coronavirus symptoms in a patient who recently came from the UK result from the more infectious UK variant. The corrective strategy is to gather different perspectives by expanding the patient's history beyond recent events or validating clinical methods rather than merely assuming.

• *Premature closure* – Consists of failing to seek more information after a diagnosis is concluded. The illness or injury may have a subsequent development, such as the occurrence of a second fracture after identifying the first. The corrective strategy involves conducting a review of the case and seeking the opinions of specialists in other fields (for instance, radiology backup in the case of a fracture). It also helps to consult objective resources – in this case, an orthopedic review that mentions a common concomitant fracture [16].

How To Think Rationally By Avoiding Biases

1. Make it a habit to research. Look for evidence that disconfirms your initial position.

2. Think of the problem on your own and create a tentative opinion before consulting others. Do this to prevent being anchored to others' ideas.

3. Think outside the box, and do not be limited by the status quo. However, before disregarding the current system or situation, evaluate how elements of the status quo may help or hurt your objectives. Avoid overstating the cost of changing from the status quo.

4. Engage with people whose positions are contrary to yours. Consult people with as many different ideas or opinions as possible, rather than focusing on a group with homogeneous positions.

5. When working with other people, avoid being defensive and argumentative when they have opinions that differ from your own. Seek a Devil's Advocate. Hear them out. Ask clarificatory and neutral questions. Do not ask leading or confrontational questions.

6. When faced with a problem defined by another, do not merely accept the initial frame in which it is construed. Try to reframe or turn the problem around to view it from other angles. Try to adopt different perspectives. Check to see if you are viewing the problem positively or negatively. Try to be objective.

7. After reframing the problem, redefine it and discard the old problem. Use the new, redefined problem to avoid digging yourself deeper into an unnecessary commitment or emotional investment. Avoid making public commitments.

8. If the problem is continuing or protracted, create a systematic or periodic review process that allows for an "out" when you need to cut your losses or admit a mistake. Keep in mind that situations may change over time, which may affect the decisions you have made and will still make.

9. To avoid being overconfident in your initial decision, always begin by considering the full range of values, the highest to the lowest possible, to avoid being anchored to one option. Imagine circumstances that will result in outcomes below your lowest estimate or above your highest estimate.

10. Document your decision-making process whenever possible to avoid changes in memory recall. Gather logs, statistics, records of procedures already undertaken, facts and details. They will help reconstruct your decision-making when it is needed during a future review.

With what we have learned about biases, why are we predisposed to making poor or bad decisions when we have the intellect to make good ones? The answer is that humans are complex beings. Our psyche is the sum of our cognitive faculties that includes our consciousness, memory, thinking, perception, judgment, and language. It enables recognition, appreciation, and imagination, processes feelings and emotions, and manifests through actions and attitudes. People will think, feel, and act differently, according to how they have processed their varied experiences, knowledge, and information. The decisions we make are relative, so some are done erroneously, while others turn out to be right.

Action Steps

In this chapter, we were introduced to several biases that we frequently encounter. The following situations involve at least one type of bias. Could you name which one? (Give it a good try before looking up the answers at the end of the chapter).

1. Pamela arrived in class just as the teacher was handing out examination questionnaires. Realizing she did not have the yellow pad paper required for the test, she whispered to her seatmate Andrew if he had an extra sheet. The teacher caught her whispering and immediately sent both Pamela and Andrew to the principal's office for cheating during an exam.

2. Francis was the third child to get sick in his family. His sisters just had the flu, and when he came down with a fever the doctor dismissed it as a matter of contagion. Francis was given medicine for the flu. After a week, however, his condition worsened. He was brought to the hospital for some tests. It was only then that the doctor

discovered that Francis had the dengue, and immediately ordered a plasma transfusion.

3. Vincent loved teaching. After he got his accreditation, he went back to the little town he grew up in and applied to teach in the same high school he went to. He was taken aback when he observed that the students were rowdy and undisciplined. They no longer stood at attention to greet the teacher and did not give due deference to the school officials. It was much better during our time, Vincent thought.

4. Elsa was in line for a promotion, along with some other employees who were similarly qualified for the position. Elsa was sure she would be granted the position, but in the end, John was awarded the promotion for his astute leadership abilities. Feeling betrayed, Elsa spread the rumor that the company was biased against women and therefore promoted a man.

5. During Cecile's first day in college, two classmates immediately showed an interest in getting to know her better. Tom was athletic and a sharp dresser, Bill looked dull and a bit nerdy. Cecile quickly favored Tom over Bill because "he looks geared for success." A decade after graduation, Tom was a salesman in Bill's billion-dollar cybernetics company.

Moving On

Tolstoy was keenly perceptive when he observed that simple-minded people are easier to teach than those who are already knowledgeable. Biases are a hindrance to the search for truth because they prevent us from accepting it even if we find it. We must, therefore, vigilantly guard against biases in ourselves and others. Unlike the six blind men of Indostan, we must diligently gather and assess all relevant information and weigh our options well before deciding.

Key Takeaways

- Confirmation bias, the most common of biases, leads us to accept information aligned with our own perception of the truth.
- First impression bias limits information processing to the opinions formed during the first encounter.
- The Dunning Kruger Effect refers to people's favorable estimation of themselves during an event or encounter.
- Fundamental Attribution Error overestimates an actor's traits while underestimating the situational factors.
- Declinism sees the past favorably and believes society's future is headed toward a decline.
- Practice caution and vigilance to avoid biases and think logically.

Solution To The Exercise

1. Fundamental Attribution Error

2. Diagnostic bias – confirmation bias

3. Declinism/Decline Bias

4.Dunning Kruger Effect

5. First Impression Bias

AFTERWORD

We live in a confusing world that is burdened not only by information overload but also opinion overload. The people we meet in person and online are only too eager to convince us of what they believe in and what they "know" to be true. We are too often swayed by the arguments they make. "He sounded so credible!" "Her statements are so convincing!" That is until the next credible and convincing argument comes along that contradicts what went before.

This little book sought to candidly and concisely unlock the secrets to logical reasoning and right thinking. Hopefully, it helps us win debates in school, present our best arguments at work, and set our relationships to rights with friends and families. But first and foremost, this book aims to help us to make the best possible decisions when facing the commonplace problems we encounter daily.

Throughout this book, we emphasized our minds' inner workings when faced with the logical proofs and the propositions they claim to support. Why is this right and that wrong? How can something that seems initially doubtful become acceptable once carefully examined?

Since humans are complex beings, our minds are sometimes predisposed to rushing to judgment and making mistakes in the process. We arrive at the wrong decisions because of biases, emotions, misconceptions, and false presumptions. We tend to commit logical errors that we could avoid if we were made aware of them.

Awareness of our propensity to commit logical errors is the first step towards correct reasoning. The second is to gain familiarity with the tools necessary to develop logical skills. This book acquainted us with these tools. First is the classical laws of logic: the laws of identity, excluded middle, non-contradiction, and sufficient reason. Next are the elements of logical reasoning, which are claims, inference, and arguments, the latter consisting of premises and conclusion. We gained acquaintance with the types of arguments, valid and invalid, sound and unsound, deductive and inductive. We came to understand why we would sometimes quarrel rather than seek the truth.

Armed with these tools, we learned the two types of errors, Formal errors violate the patterns of argument construction and render the argument invalid. Informal errors are mistakes in reasoning, called fallacies, that make an argument unsound. We then scrutinized six common types of biases that hijack our thinking process. Finally, we discovered ways to avoid these logical errors to arrive at better decisions.

Now that we have the fundamentals of logical thinking, we need to practice them if we are to benefit the most from this knowledge. Reading the book is easy. Applying what we learn from it is like learning to ride a bike. Our first clumsy attempts will meet with bumps and scrapes as gravity pulls us back to old and familiar habits. But like biking, once you learn how to do it, you will never forget it. Between start and finish, what is indispensable is practice, practice, practice. Recall the theory. Apply it to real-life situations. Learn from it. And at the next encounter, use it. That is the secret of learning how to think rationally to make logical decisions.

ONE FINAL WORD FROM US

If this book has helped you in any way, we'd appreciate it if you left a review on Amazon. Reviews are the lifeblood of our business. We read every single one and incorporate your feedback in developing future book projects.

To leave a review, simply go to: smarturl.it/clfr

(Or scan the code with your camera)

CONTINUING YOUR JOURNEY

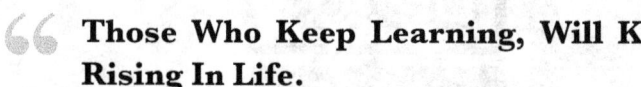 **Those Who Keep Learning, Will Keep Rising In Life.**

— CHARLIE MUNGER (BILLIONAIRE, INVESTOR, AND WARREN BUFFET'S BUSINESS PARTNER)

The most successful people in life are those who enjoy learning and asking questions, understanding themselves and the world around them.

In our Thinknetic newsletter we'll share with you our best thinking improvement tips and tricks to help you become even more successful in life.

It's 100% free and you can unsubscribe at any time.

Besides, you'll hear first about our new releases and get the chance to receive them for free or highly discounted.

As a bonus, you'll get our bestselling book *Critical Thinking In A Nutshell* & 2 thinking improvement sheets completely for free.

Go to thinknetic.net to sign up for free!

(Or simply scan the code with your camera)

THE TEAM BEHIND THINKNETIC

Michael Meisner, Founder and CEO

When Michael got into publishing books on Amazon, he found that his favorite topic - the thinking process and its results, is tackled in a much too complex and unengaging way. Thus, he set himself up to make his ideal a reality: books that are informative, entertaining, and can help people achieve success by thinking things through.

This ideal became his passion and profession. He built a team of like-minded people and is in charge of the strategic part and brand orientation, as he continues to improve and extend his business.

Diana Spoiala, Publishing Manager

From idea to print, there is a process involving researching and designing the book, writing and editing it, and providing it with the right covers. Diana oversees this process and ensures the quality of each book. Outside work, she dedicates most of her time cultivating her innate love for reading and writing literature, poetry, and philosophy.

Theresa Datinguinoo, Research and Outline Mastermind

Theresa derives "immense satisfaction from putting together ideas to provide a solid framework for an engaging story and seeing the final product come to life." Her professional background is in human resources management and psychology, but she has always enjoyed writing articles and blog posts about any subject.

Doris Lam, Senior Content Editor

Doris has been editing print media since 2005 as the Chief Copy Editor and Program Coordinator for several environmental agencies. She is committed to helping writers achieve clarity, always up for the challenge of making everyone's writing a masterpiece. For more information about Doris's great work, visit www. dorissiu.com.

Nerina Badalic, Senior Content Editor

Throughout the years, Nerina wrote articles, short stories, and songs. As an editor, she helps authors bring out the best in them to produce manuals, thesis, articles, and books that are valuable and useful to the readers. Nerina continues to explore the arts that surround the world of words: communication, marketing, design, music, and photography.

Francesca Scotti-Goetz, Newsletter Writer and Social Media Community Manager

An observer first and a copywriter second, Francesca has a passion for the intersection of art with humanity; social issues with media; thinking with creativity. She spends her weekends in Amsterdam with a camera and a notebook, and her weekdays harnessing her discoveries to effectively engage with Thinknetic's worldwide community.

Contributors:

David Brant Yu

David is committed to carefully reviewing the profiles of the many aspiring writers for Thinknetic, ensuring that the most skilled and talented ones join the team. His voracious reading habit and interests in philosophy and current affairs help him carry out his work critically. David enjoys his spare time doing freelance copyediting and English tutoring.

Evangeline Obiedo

Evangeline completes our books' journey to getting published. She pays attention to all the details, making sure that every book is properly formatted. Her love for learning extends into the real world - she loves traveling and experiencing new places and cultures.

REFERENCES

1. To Understand Reasoning Is To First Understand Logic

1. Bobzien, S. (2020) "Ancient Logic", In E.N. Zalta (ed.), *The Stanford Encyclopedia of Philosophy*, https://plato.stanford.edu/archives/sum2020/entries/logic-ancient/
2. Kraus, J. 2015 *Rhetoric in European Culture and Beyond.* Charles University in Prague.
3. Patterson, R. (2020) "7 Ways to Improve Your Critical Thinking Skills." *College Info Geek.*https://collegeinfogeek.com/improve-critical-thinking-skills/

2. Reason Through Arguments

1. Schwarz, B.B. and Asterhan, C. (2010) Argumentation and Reasoning. In K. Littleton, C. Wood, and J.Kleine Staarman (Eds.), *Elsevier Handbook of Educational Psychology: New Perspectives on Learning and Teaching.* Elsevier Press
2. Dowden, B.H. (2017) *Logical Reasoning.* Open Library, California State University,https://www.csus.edu/indiv/d/dowdenb/4/logical-reasoning-archives/Logical-Reasoning-2020-05-15.pdf
3. "Argument mapping" (2020) HKU Philosophy Department, University of Hong Kong. htthttps://www.csus.edu/indiv/d/dowdenb/4/logical-reasoning-archives/Logical-Reasoning-2020-05-15.pdfhtthttps://www.csus.edu/indiv/d/dowdenb/4/logical-reasoning-archives/Logical-Reasoning-2020-05-15.pdf%20and%20involve%20extended%20reasoning
4. Schutt, R.K. (2018) *Investigating the Social World: The Process and Practice of Research.* SAGE Publications
5. Bradford, A. (2017) "Deductive Reasoning vs Inductive Reasoning". *Live Science.*https://www.livescience.com/21569-deduction-vs-induction.html

6. "Deductive and Inductive Arguments" (2020) *Internet Encyclopedia of Philosophy.* ISSN 2161-0002.https://iep.utm.edu/ded-ind/
7. "Validity and Invalidity, Soundness and Unsoundness" (2020) *An Introduction to Philosophy.* Stanford University. https://web.stanford.edu/~bobonich/terms.concepts/terms.conc.main.html
8. DeMichele, T. (2017, June 15) "The Different Types of Reasoning Methods Explained and Compared". *Fact/Myth.* http://factmyth.com/the-different-types-of-reasoning-methods-explained-and-compared/
9. Schmidt, G. (2014) "Simple Answers" *Edge.*https://www.edge.org/response-detail/25484
10. Cohen, P. (2011, June 14) "Reason seen more as weapon than path to truth." *The New York Times.*https://www.nytimes.com/2011/06/15/arts/people-argue-just-to-win-scholars-assert.html
11. Mercier, H. & Sperber, D. (2011) Why do humans reason? Arguments for an Argumentative Theory. *Behavioral and Brain Sciences*, 34(2): 57-74
12. Kraus, J. 2015 *Rhetoric in European Culture and Beyond.* Charles University in Prague, p.6
13. Kraus, J. 2015 *Rhetoric in European Culture and Beyond.* Charles University in Prague.

3. The Culprit Of Bad Reasoning: Our Logical Errors And Biases

1. Walls, J. (2009). *Half Broke Horses: A True-Life Novel.* United States: Scribner.
2. Kim V. (2016, October 10) Stereotypes, Bias, Prejudice, and Discrimination: Oh My! *Psych Learning Curve: Where Psychology and Education Connect.* American Psychological Association.http://psychlearningcurve.org/stereotypes-bias-prejudice-and-discrimination/
3. JD (2021) Three Ways to Spot Logical Fallacies. *Sources of Insight.*https://sourcesofinsight.com/3-ways-to-spot-logical-fallacies/

4. Demystifying The So-Called Formal Logical Errors

1. Pevernagie, E. (2007) *Life Quotes and Paintings*.https://www.wattpad. com/554136351-life-quotes-and-paintings-of-erik-pevernagie
2. Ri, Y-S. 2017 'Modus Ponents and Modus Tollens: Their Validity /Invalidity in Natural language Arguments.' *Studies in Logic, Grammar and Rhetoric*. Vol 50, Issue 63, pp. 253-267.
3. Eschner, K. (2016, December 30) "The Story of the Real Canary in the Coal Mine," *Smithsonian Magazine*. https://www.smithsonianmag. com/smart-news/story-real-canary-coal-mine-180961570/#:https://www.smithsonianmag.com/smart-news/ story-real-canary-coal-mine-180961570/#:~:text=On%20this% 20day%20in%201986,gases%20before%20they%20hurt% 20humans.&text=If%20the%20animal%20became%20ill,a% 20canary%20Haldane's%20suggested%20solution%3F
4. Ri, Y-S. 2017 'Modus Ponents and Modus Tollens: Their Validity /Invalidity in Natural language Arguments.' *Studies in Logic, Grammar and Rhetoric*. Vol 50, Issue 63, pp. 253-267.
5. Mosley, A. & Baltazar, E. (2019) *An Introduction to Logic: From Everyday Life to Formal Systems*. Open Educational Resources: Textbooks, Smith College, Northampton, MA.https://scholarworks. smith.edu/textbooks/1
6. Mosley, A. & Baltazar, E. (2019) *An Introduction to Logic: From Everyday Life to Formal Systems*. Open Educational Resources: Textbooks, Smith College, Northampton, MA.https://scholarworks. smith.edu/textbooks/1
7. Eschner, K. (2016, December 30) "The Story of the Real Canary in the Coal Mine," *Smithsonian Magazine*.https://www.smithsonianmag. com/smart-news/story-real-canary-coal-mine-180961570/#:~: text=On%20this%20day%20in%201986,gases%20before% 20they%20hurt%20humans.&text=If%20the%20animal% 20became%20ill,a%20canary%20Haldane's%20suggested% 20solution%3F
8. Rice, S.M. (2015) Indispensable Logic: Using the Logical Fallacy of the Undistributed Middle As a Mitigation Tool. *Akron Law Journals*, 43(1):3

5. The Informal Logical Errors We Experience Everyday

1. Funder, D.C. (1987) Errors and Mistakes: Evaluating the Accuracy of Social Judgment. *Psychological Bulletin*, 10(2):75-90
2. Nikolova, H., Lamberton, C., & Haws, K.L. (2016) Haunts or helps from the past: Understanding the effect of recall on current self-control. *Psychology*, 26(2): 245-256.
3. Lerner, J.S., Li, Y., Valdesolo, P., & Kassam, K. (2015) Emotion and Decision Making. *Annual Review of Psychology.* 66:799-823
4. Finnell, M. (Producer) & Dante, J. (Director) (1984) *Gremlins*. [Motion picture]. United States: Warner Bros. and Amblin Entertainment
5. "About Dairy Cows" (2021) *Compassion in World Farming*. https://www.ciwf.com/farmed-animals/cows/dairy-cows/
6. Damer, T.E. (2009) *Attacking Faulty Reasoning: A Practical Guide to Fallacy-Free Arguments, 6th edition*. Belmont, CA: Wadsworth Cengage Learning
7. Conroy, J. (2007, September 24). "Probing Question: Is the Farmers' Almanac accurate?" *Penn State News*. Penn State. https://news.psu.edu/story/141165/2007/09/24/research/probing-question-farmers-almanac-accurate#:~:text=The%20Farm-ers'%20Almanac's %20Web%20site,months%20in%20advance%20for%20seven
8. "History of the Old Farmer's Almanac" (2016, August 14) *The Old Farmer's Almanac*. https://www.almanac.com/content/history-old-farmers-almanac#
9. *The Old Farmer's Almanac* (2021, February 16) The Old Farmer's Almanac. Retrieved 16 February 2021 from https://www.almanac.com/
10. Van Eemeren, F.H. (2010) *Strategic Maneuvering in Argumentative Discourse: Extending the Pragma-dialectical Theory of Argumentation*. John Benjamin Publishing.
11. Frank, R.B. (2017) Hacksaw Ridge; The Conscientious Objector; The Unlikeliest Hero: The Story of Desmond T. Doss, Conscientious Objector Who Won His Nation's Highest Military Honor. *Journal of American History*, 104(1): 301-305.
12. Mechanic, B., Permut, D., Benedict, T., Currie, P., Davie, B., Oliver, B., & Johnson, W.D. (Producers) & Gibson, M. (Director) (2016) *Hacksaw Ridge* [Motion picture]. United States: Summit Entertainment and others

13. Sathe, V. (2017) Smaller But Not Secondary: Evidence of Rodents in Archaeological Context in India. *Ancient Asia*, 8:6, pp.1-20, DOI: http://doi.org/10.5334/aa.131

14. Zakir Hossain, M. (2009) "Why is interest prohibited in Islam? A statistical justification." *Humanomics*, 25(4): 241-253

15. Mowrey Admin (2017, February 14) "The Rule of 13: Why Isn't There a 13th Floor?" *Mowrey Elevator.*http://www.mowreyelevator.com/industry-updates/rule-13-isnt-13th-floor/

16. Magnan, J. (2018) Appeal to Ignorance. *Journal of International Advanced Otology*, 14(3):504-505. DOI: 10.5152/iao.2018.141118

17. Smith, W. (2021) "Flag of Western Australia." *Britannica.* Encyclopedia Britannica, Inc.https://www.britannica.com/topic/flag-of-Western-Australia

18. Taleb, N.N. (2007, April 22) "The Black Swan: The Impact of the Highly Improbable". *The New York Times.*https://www.nytimes.com/2007/04/22/books/chapters/0422-1st-tale.html

19. Suárez-Lledó, J. (2011) The Black Swan: The Impact of the Highly Improbable. *Academy of Management Journal.* 25(2):87-90, doi:10.5465/amp.25.2.87

20. TSU Department of Philosophy (2021) "Begging the Question," Texas State University.https://www.txstate.edu/philosophy/resources/fallacy-definitions/Begging-the-Question.html#:~:text=The%20fallacy%20of%20begging%20the,called%20arguing%20in%20a%20circle

21. Grote, G. (1872) *Aristotle.* John Murray.

22. Dowden, B.H. (2020) *Logical Reasoning.* Philosophy Department, California State University Sacramento

23. Feige, K. {Producer} & Russo, A. & Russo, J. (Directors) (2018) *Avengers: Infinity War* [Motion Picture] United States: Marvel Studios.

24. Dowden, B.H. (2020) *Logical Reasoning.* Philosophy Department, California State University Sacramento

25. Legg, T.J. (2020, Feb. 26) "'Gateway Drug' or 'Natural Healer?' 5 Common Cannabis Myths." *Healthline.*https://www.healthline.com/health/is-marijuana-a-gateway-drug

26. Lupoli, M.J., Jampol, L., & Oveis, C. (2017) Lying because we care: Compassion increases prosocial lying. *Journal of Experimental Psychology: General.* 146(7): 1026–1053

27. Arkes, H. R., & Blumer, C. (1985), The psychology of sunk costs. *Organizational Behavior and Human Decision Processes*, 35: 124-1401026-1042

28. Roth, S., Robbert, T., & Straus, L. (2015) On the sunk-cost effect in economic decision-making: A meta-analytic review. *Business Research.* 8: 99-138

29. "Sunk Cost Fallacy" (2020) *Behavioral Economics.*https://www.behavioraleconomics.com/resources/mini-encyclopedia-of-be/sunk-cost-fallacy/

30. Erickson, A. & Vaidya, A.J. (2011) *Logical & Critical Reasoning: Conceptual Foundations and Techniques of Evaluation.* United States. Kendall Hunt.

31. Johnson, C. & Hall-Lande, J. (2005/06) "Growing Up in Foster Care: Carolyn's Story." *Impact.* 19(1): 1,36

32. Lewinski, M. (2011) Towards a Critique-Friendly Approach to the Straw Man Fallacy Evaluation. *Argumentation.* 25:469. DOI: https://doi.org/10.1007/s10503-011-9227-6

33. Damer, T.E. (2009) *Attacking Faulty Reasoning: A Practical Guide to Fallacy-Free Arguments, 6th edition.* Belmont, CA: Wadsworth Cengage Learning

34. Wood, R. (2002) Critical Thinking.https://www.robinwood.com/Democracy/GeneralEssays/CriticalThinking.pdf

35. Chen, J. (2021, February 23) "A Mom's Research (Part 2): Texas Freezing and Global Warming." *The Epoch Times.* https://www.theepochtimes.com/a-moms-research-part-2-texas-freezing-and-global-warming_3705225.html?utm_source=pushengage

36. Vaidya, A. & Erickson, A. (2011) *Logical and Critical Reasoning.* Kendall Hunt, p.43

6. Making The Change: How Can We Become Rational Thinkers?

1. Tolstoy, L. (1894) *The Kingdom of God is Within You.* Cassell Publishing Company

2. Saxe, J.G. (1872) "The Blind Men and the Elephant," https://en.wikisource.org/wiki/The_poems_of_John_Godfrey_Saxe/The_Blind_Men_and_the_Elephant

3. Nickerson, R.S. (1998) Confirmation Bias: A Ubiquitous Phenomenon in Many Guises. *Review of General Psychology,* 2(2): 175-220

4. Patterson, R. (2020) "7 Ways to Improve Your Critical Thinking Skills." *College Info Geek.* https://collegeinfogeek.com/improve-critical-thinking-skills/

5. Lim, K.H., Benbasat, I., & Ward, L.M. (2000) The Role of Multimedia in Changing First Impression Bias, *Information Systems Research*, 11(2): 115-136

6. Okten, I.O. (2018, January 13) "Studying First Impressions: What to Consider?" *Association for Psychological Science.*https://www.psychologicalscience.org/observer/studying-first-impressions-what-to-consider

7. Kruger, J. & Dunning, D. (1999) Unskilled and unaware of it: How difficulties in recognizing one's own incompetence lead to inflated self-assessments. *Journal of Personality and Social Psychology*, 77(6): 1121-1134

8. Kruger, J. & Dunning, D. (1999) Unskilled and unaware of it: How difficulties in recognizing one's own incompetence lead to inflated self-assessments. *Journal of Personality and Social Psychology*, 77(6): 1121-1134

9. Berry, Z. (2015) Explanations and Implications of the Fundamental Attribution Error: A Review and Proposal. *Journal of Integrated Social Sciences*, 5(1): 44-57

10. Healy, P. (2017, June 8) "The Fundamental Attribution Error: What It Is and How to Avoid It." *Harvard Business School Online.* https://online.hbs.edu/blog/post/the-fundamental-attribution-error

11. Elchardus, M. (2017) Declinism and Populism. *Clingendael Spectator 3*, 71:2.https://spectator.clingendael.org/pub/2017/3/_/pdf/IS-2017-3-elchardus.pdf

12. The Decision Lab (2021) "Why we feel the past is better compared to what the future holds." *The Decision Lab.* https://thedecision-lab.com/biases/declinism/

13. Banerjee, A., Pluddemann, A., & O'Sullivan, J. (2017) "Diagnostic Suspicion Bias," *Catalogue of Bias.* https://catalogofbias.org/biases/diagnostic-suspicion-bias/

14. Wellbery, C. (2011) Flaws in Clinical Reasoning: A Common Cause of Diagnostic Error. *American Family Physician*, 84(9):1042-1044.

15. Wellbery, C. (2011) Flaws in Clinical Reasoning: A Common Cause of Diagnostic Error. *American Family Physician*, 84(9):1042-1044.

16. Wellbery, C. (2011) Flaws in Clinical Reasoning: A Common Cause of Diagnostic Error. *American Family Physician*, 84(9):1042-1044.

DISCLAIMER

The information contained in this book and its components, is meant to serve as a comprehensive collection of strategies that the author of this book has done research about. Summaries, strategies, tips and tricks are only recommendations by the author, and reading this book will not guarantee that one's results will exactly mirror the author's results.

The author of this book has made all reasonable efforts to provide current and accurate information for the readers of this book. The author and its associates will not be held liable for any unintentional errors or omissions that may be found.

The material in the book may include information by third parties. Third party materials comprise of opinions expressed by their owners. As such, the author of this book does not assume responsibility or liability for any third party material or opinions.

Printed in the USA
CPSIA information can be obtained
at www.ICGtesting.com
LVHW042002251123
764838LV00002B/355